Aeronautical Cartography

Conforti, Facundo Jorge
   Cartografía aeronáutica / Facundo Jorge Conforti. - 1a ed . - Mar del Plata : Facundo Jorge Conforti, 2019.
   200 p. ; 21 x 14 cm. - (How does it work? ; 15)

1. Aviación. 2. Escuela Piloto. 3. Aviones. I. Título.
CDD 629.13

Fecha de Catalogación: 02/10/2018

Aviación en Simples Pasos
HOW DOES IT WORK?
1ra Edición.

Facundo Conforti, 2022.

Queda hecho el deposito que establece la Ley 11.723.
Libro de edición Argentina.
No se permite la reproducción total o parcial, el almacenamiento,
el alquiler, la transmisión o la transformación de este libro,
en cualquier formato o por cualquier medio, sea electrónico
o mecánico, mediante fotocopias, digitalización u otros métodos,
sin el permiso previo y escrito del editor. Su infracción está
penada por las Leyes 11.723 y 25.446.

Preface

Welcome to the most successful collection in America. In this book, we will cover one of the most relevant topics for training professional pilots. We will dedicate our pages to understanding aeronautical cartography for IFR flights. Based on the world's leading manufacturer of aeronautical cartography, JEPPESEN SANDERSON Inc., we will analyse all types of charts that can be presented in our profession during a professional flight.

Today, the most important airlines in the world base their operations on the cartography published by JEPPESEN and constantly train their pilots to understand these documents, favouring the safety of air operations.

The geography of our planet is very complex and requires a personalized design for every airport in the world. This concept forces aeronautical cartography to be constantly updated and forces pilots to improve themselves at all times for a correct understanding of the procedures.

Capt. Facundo Conforti

Main

Introduction   07

Chapter 1 Airports

Airport Information charts   17
Analysis and Symbology Sao Paulo (SGBR)   20
Taxi Operations (SBGR)   26
Analysis and Symbology Mendoza (SAME)   28
Hot Spots   30
Analysis and Symbology México (MMMX)   32
Low Visibility Taxi   39

Chapter 2 Instrumental departures

General information   45
Analysis and Symbology Buenos Aires (SABE)   46
Briefing SID (standard instrumental departure)   50
Flight operation SID SABE   53
SID for engine failure (EOSID)   55
Overview SID   58
SID over mountains   60

Chapter 3 In flight

General information   69
Cartographic Symbology   71
Area charts   79
Practical Analysis   83

Chapter 4 Arrivals

General information	93
Analysis and Symbology Barcelona (LEBL)	94
Operation Barcelona (LEBL)	97
Analysis and Symbology Buenos Aires (SABE)	98
Operation Buenos Aires (SABE)	100
Analysis and Symbology Salta (SASA)	101
Overview STAR	106
Airport Familiarization (SBGR)	107
Operation in MEXICO (MMMX)	109
Operation in LIMA (SPJC)	112

Chapter 5 Approach

General information	121
Analysis and Symbology VOR charts	123
Analysis and Symbology NDB charts	139
Analysis and Symbology LOC charts	145
Analysis and Symbology mixed charts	149
Analysis and Symbology ILS charts	158

Abbreviations	177
Symbols	187

Introduction

When we talk about aeronautical cartography, we refer to a large number of chart designs and models, whether visual or instrumental. The aeronautical authority of each country is responsible for preparing its own charts in its cartographic department (if it has one). This information is taken by different mapping manufacturers worldwide and they adapt this information to their own models by making the corrections they deem necessary. In our particular case, we will base our examples on the world's leading manufacturer of aeronautical cartography, JEPPESEN SANDERSON Inc. www.jeppesen.com

Aeronautical mapping is an extensive topic since it involves different kinds of charts, such as:

- Visual navigation charts
- Instrumental navigation charts
- Airport information charts
- Airspace information charts
- Instrumental departure charts
- Instrumental arrival charts
- Instrumental approach charts
- Visual approach charts

In the course of this manual, we will go through all these charts and know their details to achieve a simple and definitive understanding of how to operate with aeronautical cartography.

Let's make a breakdown of each of these groups of charts and analyze their variables according to the correct order in which they would be used in flight. Let's see:

 Airport information charts involve a series of data and plans of the architecture of each terminal as well as information on special operations and restrictions. In this group of charts, we will find very important information such as: taxiways, parking positions, information about the runway and the vicinity of the aerodrome, communication frequencies and descriptions of special procedures, specific to each airport. This mapping group is the starting point of an IFR flight and is the first contact of the pilot when arriving at the aircraft. These charts will take the pilot to the runway in use after having traveled through the different taxiways throughout the airport. When it's time for takeoff, we will move on to the next chart.

Departures charts

The departure charts arrive immediately after the takeoff of the aircraft and offer the pilot a detailed description of what he must do after leaving the airport terminal. These charts are the pilot's first contact with an instructive "plane" or "map" where he can find all the necessary information for his departure, such as: courses, radio aid and communications frequencies, minimum and maximum altitudes, speeds, noise attenuation procedures, waypoints, nearby airports and other information relevant to his departure until he reaches its endpoint, the moment just where this departure chart ends and starts the next one, the navigation chart or route map.

Routes charts

Here, the last point of the departure chart becomes the first starting point of the instrumental navigation chart. From here, the flight route to the destination begins. In this group of charts, the pilot can find information about: courses, distances, flight levels, radio aids, communication frequencies, restrictions, nearby airports and routes that deviate to them, information about restricted and/or prohibited airspace, and other information relevant to all navigation throughout one or more countries.

Arrivals charts

Arriving at the last point of the route, the pilot finds the entry point to the terminal area of his destination airport. From here, it begins his journey to the airport, descending to the indicated altitude and to the final point before entering the approach for the runway of the course. In this group of charts, we will find information about: courses, altitudes, waypoint, nearby airports, communication frequencies, radio aids, and other relevant information to enter the terminal area.

Approach charts

After finishing a chart of entry, the pilot will be at the starting point of the instrumental approach or IFR procedure. From this point, the route diagrammed on the chart will begin which will take you to a minimum distance and altitude before making contact with the runway, or in some particular cases, will take you until you land on the runway even if there is no horizontal visibility. In this type of chart, we can find information about: courses, communication frequencies, radio aids, minimum altitudes, visibility, special procedures, details of the runway and its approach systems, obstacle information, contingency plan in case of some type of fault typical of the airport or due to degradation of weather conditions, and other information relevant to the approach and landing.

Airports information charts

Finally, and after landing, the pilot will again make use of the airport information charts in order to know the type of running that will take us to his final parking position.

Considering the enormous diversity of charts in each of the aforementioned groups, we will dedicate an exclusive chapter to each of them where we will learn all the relevant details to the daily operation of aeronautical cartography.

Before starting the first group of aeronautical cartography, we must know the main navigation systems on which all these aforementioned charts are based. Let's see.

Discarding airport information mapping, which is based on visual references such as signs painted on the asphalt or indicator posters, the rest of the mapping groups are based on navigation principles on which a diagram is formed that the pilot must follow with the aircraft.

The main navigation systems on which these groups of charts are based are:

- **NAVAID** *(Navigation Aids)*
- **PBN** *(Performance Based Navigation)*

NAVAID: It is the traditional navigation system that involves radio aids and/or markers such as Distance Measuring Equipment (DME), Non-Directional Beacons (NDB), Tactical Air Navigation (TACAN) systems, Very High Frequency (VHF) Omni-Directional Range (VOR) systems, VOR Test Facilities (VOT), and some combinations of these. On an other note, the ILS (instrument landing system) system is part of the NAVAID system but is considered as a final approach system and not navigation.

Currently, the NAVAID system is the most popular and used by general or small aviation. This navigation aid system is distributed throughout the territory of a country in order to function as links between airports forming radio routes. In medium-sized airports we find navigation aids provided by the instrumental approach service to a certain runway. The more equipped the airport is with radio navigation aids, the greater its category and vice versa.

PBN: The PBN system or Performance Based Navigation system, operates independently of conventional radio aids that are physically installed on the ground. Due to the NAVAIDS systems' independence the pilot is able to conduct continuous air operations within a given airspace that is often different from the airspace that a NAVAID operation would transit. PBN operations are designed for in-flight operations, departures, approaches and in certain airspaces.

The aeronautical authorities have certain requirements for the PBN operation of both the aircraft and the companies that desire to operate such a system. The two categories that make up this system are based on how accurate GPS data is:**RNAV** *(Area Navigation)*

RNAV *(Area Navigation)*
RNP *(Required Navigation Performance)*

The RNAV system allows you to make more direct routes saving fuel, as well as control over assigning lower minimum altitudes without the need to maintain a certain minimum flight level for the reception of the VOR when you are not dependent on it.

As a system based on GPS information, it is necessary to improve signal reception, as a result, there is a system known as WAAS (Wide Area Augmentation System). By having ground stations produce a corrected message and transmit it to the aircraft through geostationary satellites, this approach maximizes the accuracy of GPS signals.. This corrective message enhances the GPS signal's precision and reduces any potential lateral deviation brought on by the ionosphere and other atmospheric factors.. Let's examine the path that the information takes before it reaches the aircraft receiver aboard the airplane.

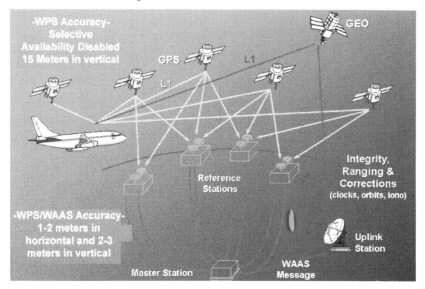

Besides, the RNP system enables more precision because it calls an on-board alert system that allows the crew to be made aware of any deviation from the planned flight path. This RNP system works in conjunction with the infrastructure and facilities of an airport equipped for this purpose. Due to its greater precision, its operation is mainly based on approaches where the required precision is higher.

It should be noted that to operate these two aforementioned systems, both the crew and the aircraft, as well as the company, must be certified and qualified.

After we've covered the various ways to navigate using various types of cartography, we will concentrate a chapter for each aforementioned group. Let's get started!

Chapter 1

Airport Information Charts

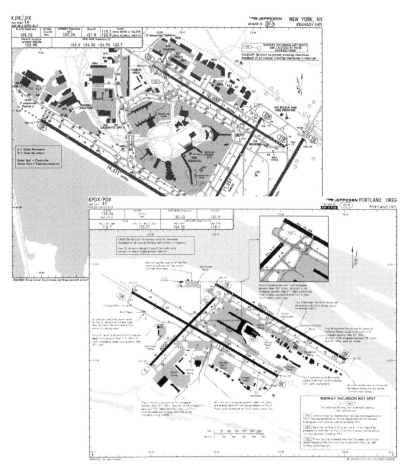

Airports
information
charts

Introduction

We know that there are thousands of airports around the world, each with a unique shape and size but also with similar technical characteristics. It would be impossible, if not impossible, to know every airport in the world and their characteristics. Besides, understanding all of the symbolism that airport mapping may present is critical, as there are hundreds of different variables between each airport where a pilot could operate.

However, among the vast amount of information and symbols found on an airport charter, there are some symbols and groups of information that are commonly shared by most airports, such as:

- Name of the city and geographical area of the aerodrome.
- The runways
- The taxiways
- Radio frequencies
- Parking positions
- Special and obstacle warnings
- Visual references
- Terminals

In most cases, this type of chart is represented in the traditional format shown below, with its position varying from vertical to horizontal while maintaining the structure of the information provided.

In both options, the chart begins with a header that provides basic information about the airport and the city where it is located. Following this, in the second section, there are radio frequencies, and depending on how many section controls each airport has, there may only be one or more radio frequencies in this area. The most relevant runways, streets, terminals and geographical information are given in the aerial picture of the region and the airport's structure. Finally, two parts with more details about the runways and information about the essential operating of the airport arrive, which may or may not go together,.

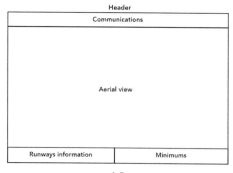

What I love most about my home is the people I share it with ♥

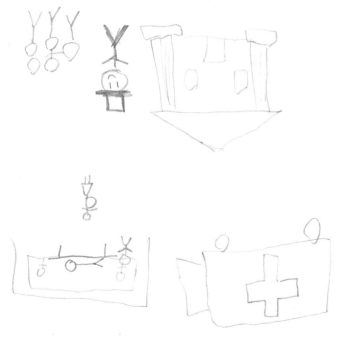

JOHNSTON & DANIEL
A DIVISION OF ROYAL LEPAGE REAL ESTATE SERVICES LTD. BROKERAGE

kimhomes.ca
416-258-8781
Alysa Kim, Sales Representative, Royal LePage/Johnston & Daniel Division, Brokerage
Not intended to solicit Sellers or Buyers currently under contract with another brokerage

KIM homes

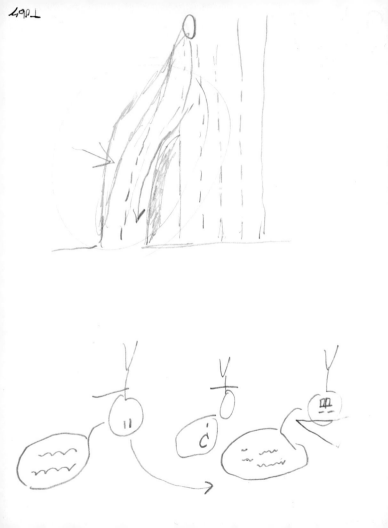

Although this format may vary depending on the airport's complexity and/or structure, the information provided will always be the same and in the same way, complying with the following scheme:

Header - Frequencies - Overview - Additional information.

In addition to the airport information charts and as a complement to them, a new cartography module emerged where the area is photographically represented in order to provide the pilot with a visual reference to use in case of not knowing the sector. They are known as panoramic charts or overview charts. This type of chart is also part of this first cartographic group that we will study, since it provides additional information about the area where it is located at the airport.

Although not all airports have this type of cartography, they are usually found in the extreme traffic airports of the largest cities in the world. A type of cartography mostly used in moments prior to the approach in order to know the area to fly over this section.

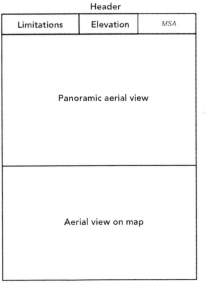

Analysis and Symbology Sao Paulo, Brazil (SBGR)

Let's start by analyzing each section of an airport charter. In this case, we will analyse Sao Paulo International Airport, Brazil.

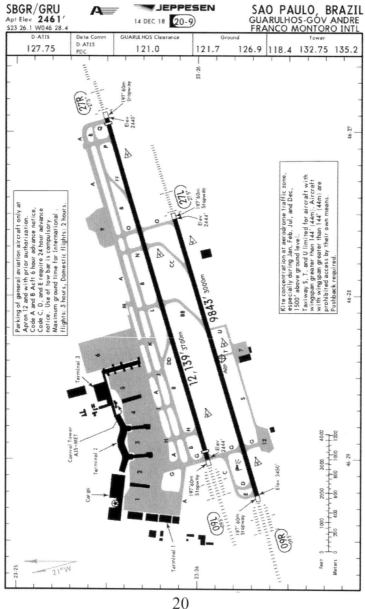

Let's carefully analyse the information provided by each section of the chart:

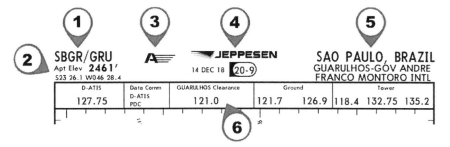

1) ICAO designation and IATA designation.

2) Elevation of the airport and geographical coordinates.

3) Airline logo.

4) Manufacturer's brand, date of creation and chart number.

5) Name of the city, country and proper name of the airport.

6) Frequencies available from all sections.

One of the advantages of this type of initial mapping is that the radio frequencies are in the correct order in which they should be used, that is: first the ATIS, then Clearance, then Ground and finally Tower. Besides, we note that in the Ground and Tower frequency tables there are more than one frequency, this may be due to two conditions. In the first instance, there may be more than one frequency to predict the failure of any of them. On the other hand, in large airports, there are the frequencies of areas, that is, Ground Norte and Ground Sur.

Let's continue with the aerial view of Sao Paulo airport:

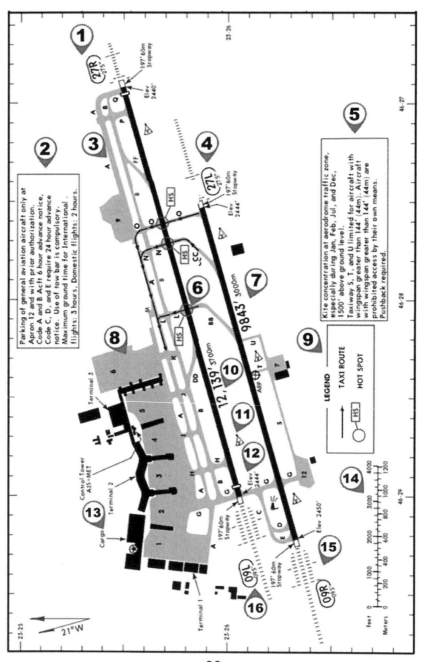

1) Runway number, course, elevation and light systems

2) Information table (information, warnings, etc.)

3) Taxiways named with chart. Example: taxiway Alfa

4) Idem point number 1

5) Idem point number 2

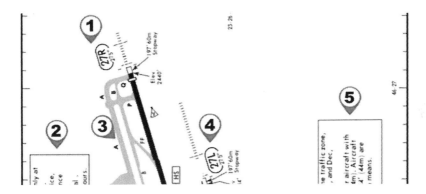

6) HOT SPOT. These Points are usually common in congested traffic airports and numerous taxiways, where there is the possibility that at the intersection of several streets or runways, the crew may be confused when taking one route or another since the streets may be together, or it can be a point of traffic congestion where there is the possibility or risk of collision.

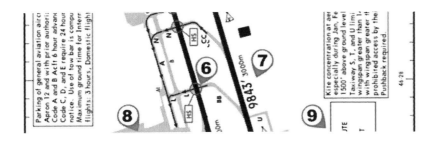

7) Runway length expressed in feet and meters.

8) Airport terminals. In this particular case and due to the magnitude of the place, each terminal is numbered for easy identification.

9) Informative table.

10) Idem point number 7.

11) Transmitter symbol.

12) Runway elevation.

13) Cargo terminal and location of the control tower.

14) Reference scale

15 and 16) Idem point number 1.

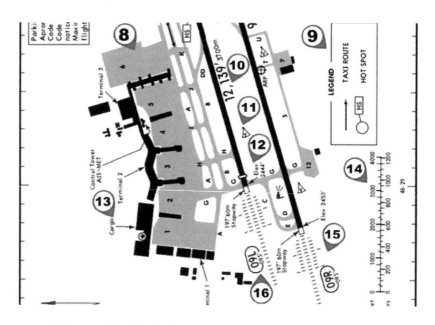

Along with this information chart from the airport, there is the second one that expands the information about the terminals and their respective parking positions. At smaller airports, these two charts are usually on the same chart. Let's look at SBGR's second chart:

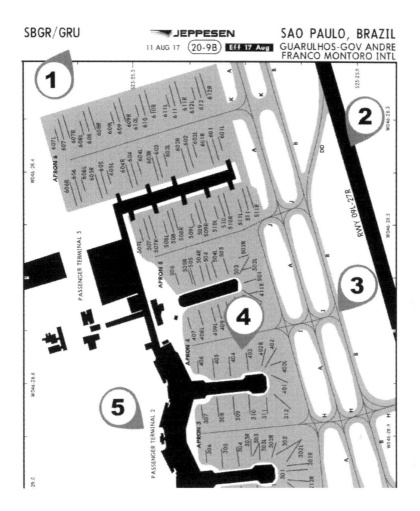

1) As in the previous chart, it begins with an airport data header, chart number, city, country and airport name.
2) As a visual reference, a fragment of the runway is represented to have knowledge of its position with respect to the streets.
3) Taxiways named with chart (A, B, C...)
4) Numbered parking positions for each airport terminal.

5) Passenger terminals assigned to different groups of parking positions.

Taxi operations (SBRG)

The use of this chart is very simple. Let's look at the following example: the aircraft lands on runway 09L, evicts it on the DD taxiway and continues along it until the intersection of B-street. Continue on B to the intersection of I Street and from there to Terminal 4 (APRON4). It has touched the parking position number 405, continue through the centre of the platform and on your left you will find the assigned position.

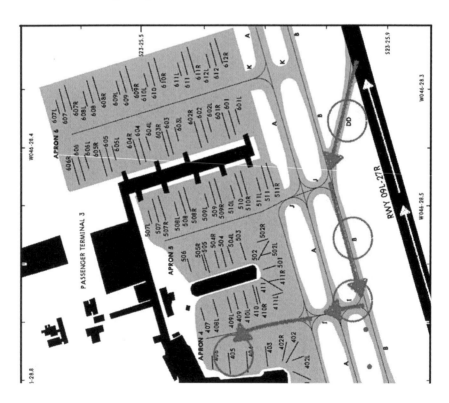

Summarizing the above concepts, we can assume that the ground operation at SAO PAULO airport (SBGR) will be based in principle on the following two charts:

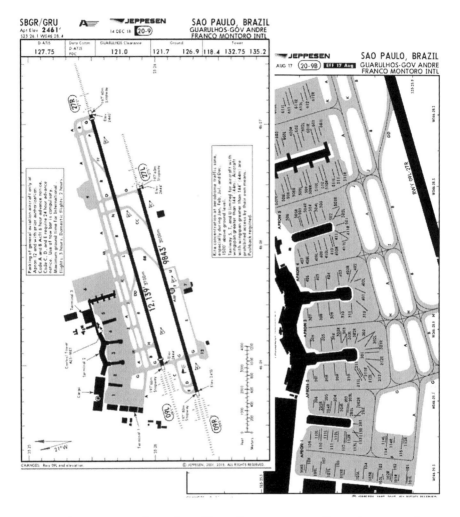

As we mentioned earlier, there are smaller airports where these two charts become one and represent all the information in the same scheme. Let's look at some examples.

Analysis and Symbology Mendoza, Argentina (SAME)

Due to the dimensions of this airport, the cartography has a simple and integrated structure compared to the previous one.

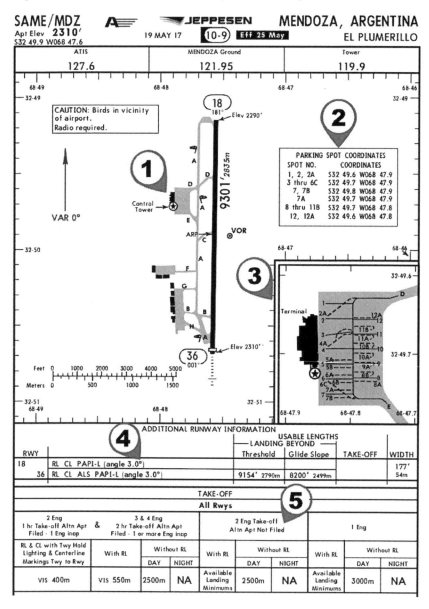

Point number one represents the airport terminal, where the control tower and the parking positions are located, but these are mentioned in an additional box (point three). In point two we find a box of geographical coordinates of each parking position.

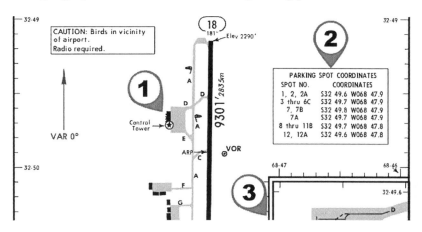

Finally, in the lower section we find the information regarding the runways (point four) and their minimums for takeoff (point five). Let's look at an example: According to the additional information on the runway, we know that runway 18 has a PAPI system with a slope of 3.0°. On the other hand, the take-off minimums report that for takeoffs of two-engine aircraft, the minimum visibility must be 2500 meters.

Hot Spots

Let's go back for a few moments to an issue of utmost importance for safe operation within an airport, HOT SPOTS. As we mentioned at SBGR airport, the hotspots are where they could be confusing and generate an incident due to collision or loss of situational awareness in the face of marginal visibility conditions. Let's look at an excerpt from the taxi chart from Lima, Peru. There are a considerable number of HOTSPOTS here in a small area of operation. Unlike the HOTSPOTS at SBGR airport, here they present a written detail clarifying word for word each of the points of conflict. Let's see:

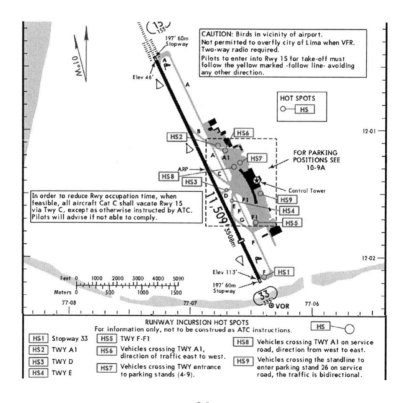

Let's look at the description and carefully analyse the charts of the taxiways:

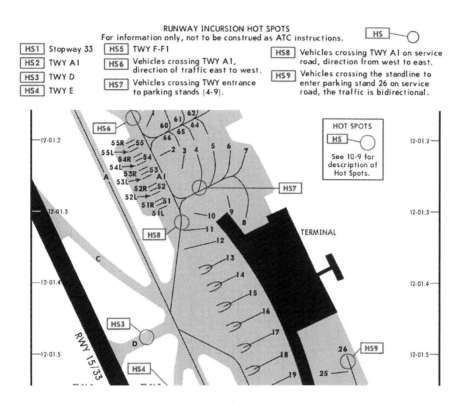

Let's take the HP7 as an example. Its description indicates that at this point there may be vehicles entering and leaving from positions 4 to 9. Let's look at another example with the HP9. Its description indicates that there may be vehicles that cross the entrance lines to the parking positions and that there is two-way traffic, which could lead to a collision.

Analysis and Symbology México (MMMX)

Having understood this concept, let's move on now to a more complete airport, welcome to Mexico Airport:

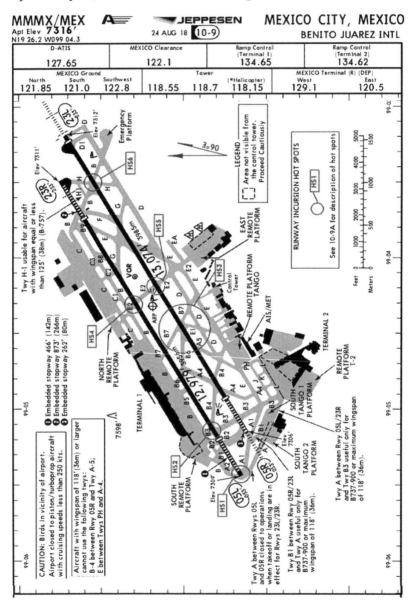

Benito Juárez International Airport, is a very interesting airport that offers endless operational possibilities. Let's analyse your main charts in more detail by sections:

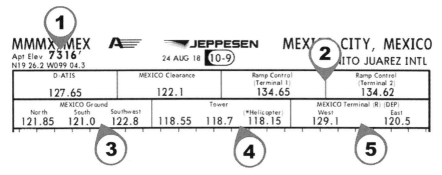

Starting with point 1, the first relevant data of this chart is the elevation of the airport, 7316FT, a very important fact.

At point 2, we find the first difference from the previous charts, a ramp or platform control divided into two sectors and each with its frequency, one for terminal 1 and the other for terminal 2. This division allows for more fluid control and with less interference.

The same concept applies to surface or taxiing frequencies, divided into "north", "south" and "south west" (point 3). Point 4, no considers this, but divides flight operations for airplanes and helicopters. Finally, in point 5, we find the "Departure Control". Here the division of the frequencies returns and they must be used according to the direction of departure, that is, if the flight is directed to the west, you must contact frequency 129.1; and if the flight is heading east, you must contact frequency 120.5.

Let's move on to the aerial view and its different sections:

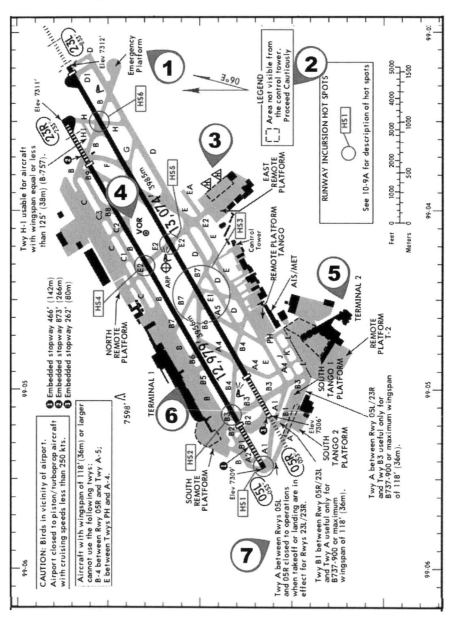

Unlike the charts seen before, here we find new points such as:

1) Emergency platform. Place intended for the resolution of conflicts such as fire, bomb threats or any other situation that could put people at risk near a passenger terminal.

2) A common warning at large airports that informs about an area "Without visibility " from the control tower and suggests a carefull operation since the taxiing assistance service would not be available.

3) A new symbol to be known, the chart H inside a triangle represents the landing area of helicopters.

4) Physical position of the VOR antenna.

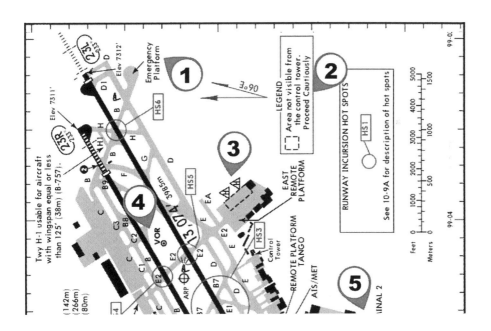

5 and 6) Terminals 1 and 2. Each of them is on one side of the runways and distant from each other. As we mentioned in previous pages, each terminal has its own frequency to maximize the flow of traffic in the running of each sector.

7) Finally, information paragraphs on this sector appear in point 7. For example: one of them warns that taxiway A between runways 05L and 05R will remain closed when takeoff operations are carried out from runways 23L and 23R. To the right of this information there is another warning indicating that the B1 taxiway between runways 05L/R will be limited to operations of B737-900 aircraft or aircraft with a maximum wingspan of 36 meters.

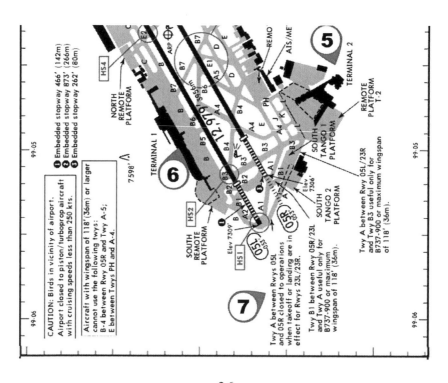

Taxi operations MMMX and SPJC

In an airport of these characteristics, taxiing operations are usually complex and careful. Taxi Clearance, or "permisos de rodaje", must contain all the streets through which the aircraft will travel from its parking position to the waiting point of the runway it is going to use. Continuing with the example of Mexico City airport, let's look at a taxiing clearance and analyse its route: in this example, the aircraft is in terminal 1, section or platform L. They tell you to take off from runway 23R and your clearance is as follows:

L–PH–E–D–H–HS R23L (hold short RWY23L)–B–HP RWY 23R

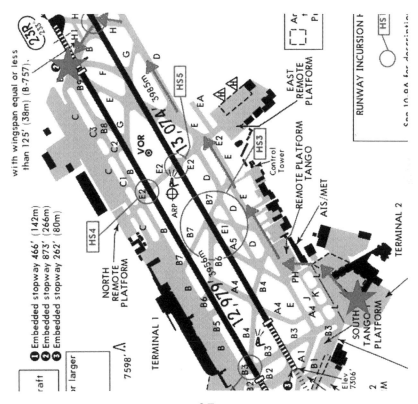

- *Have you managed the taxi clearance to runway 23R?*

Don't be discouraged if it has been difficult for you, these airports with numerous streets and intersections are among the most complex in the world. Let's look at a smaller and simpler one, Lima airport, Peru. The aircraft is on the F1 platform and must take off from runway 15. The taxi clearance is as follows:

F1 – A1 – A - HP RWY 15

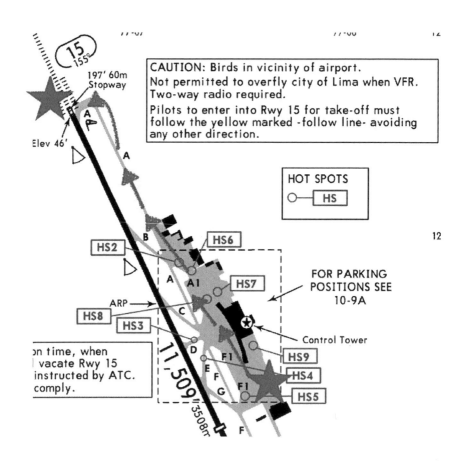

Low Visibility Taxi (LVT)

Taxi operations can be affected by reduced visibility, to the point that disables the pilot to observe the taxiways while operating the plane. Although in the face of these weather conditions, operations are canceled, at certain airports there is the possibility of having a taxiway chart for low visibility.

LVT operations are procedures that are carried out on a certain area of the airport and not on all its streets. LVT charts offer a safe route until you reach one of its runways and then continue with a takeoff with low visibility or LVTO (low visibility take off).

Now let's look at some examples of LVT charts and learn how to operate with them. Let's go to Buenos Aires, Argentina, and see a procedure at Ezeiza International Airport.

The header describes that it is a "Low Visibility Taxi Routes" procedure for a visibility of less than 400Mts of RVR. Followed by this, in point 2 we find the row of frequencies, similar to the previous ones. In point 3, a box with the symbology of this chart.

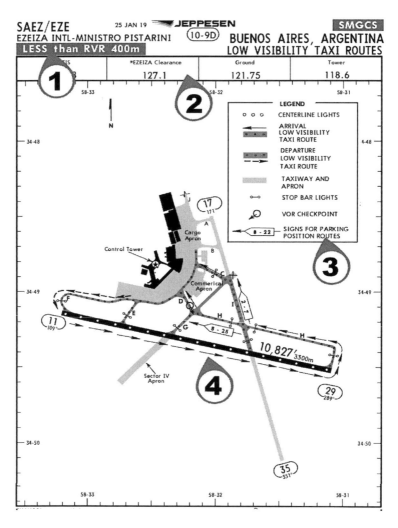

And finally, in point 4 the description of the LVT route indicated by an arrow path. Let's take a closer look at this:

The arrow path indicates a whole route from the different parking positions to runway 11 and vice versa. Whether to start the flight or by ending it with the running after landing, this charts from LVT details your route through the different areas of the airport.

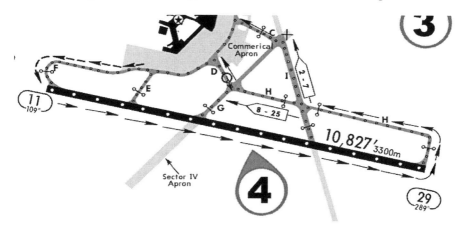

Note that the LVT procedure is only provided for runway 11 and for the rest of the runways no procedure is described. This is because AWO procedures are usually associated with a runway with an ILS CAT II-III system and all its equipment, which not only allows approaches with reduced visibility but also taxiing and even takeoffs with low visibility.

Let's look at one more example of LVT procedures and its respective mapping. We cross the Andes Mountain Range and reach the City of Santiago de Chile, Chile. This airport has parallel runways and an LVT procedure for two of its runways. In addition, it has two HSs! Let's see:

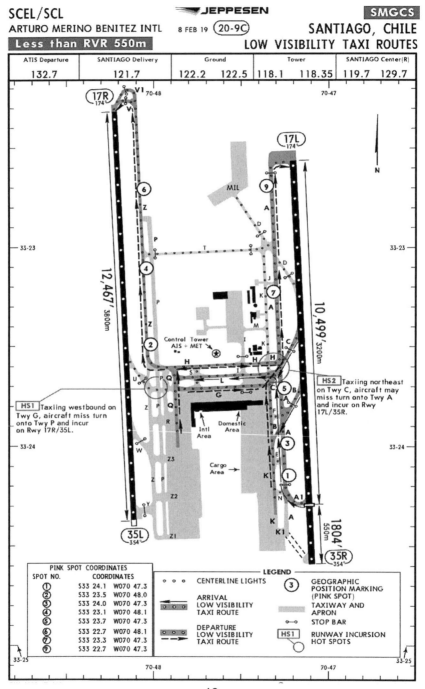

Chapter 2

Standard Instrumental Departure (SID)

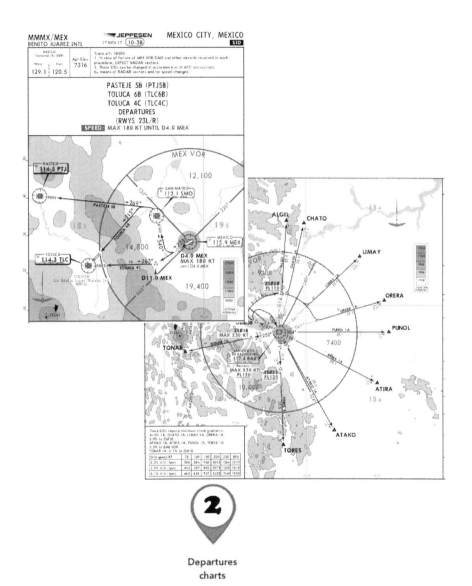

Departures
charts

Introduction

Similar to the previous charts (airport information), the SIDs represent a diagram of the area where the aircraft would operate if you want to use a standardized departure. Like the previous charts, SIDs have a format divided into different sections. This format can be presented both vertically and horizontally depending on the information. Let's see:

The header maintains the same format as the previous charts. The aerial view has similar characteristics but with additional information such as the MSA. The lower section consists of information related to the climb and the points to follow until you reach the airway.

Unlike airport information charts seen on previous pages, in SIDs it is uncommon to find a radio frequency section since they were clarified in the previous charts.

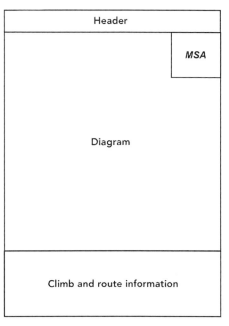

This chart format is flexible concerning the position of the information, and its location may vary in different dialog boxes.

Analysis and Symbology Buenos Aires (SABE)

Let's look at a SID from the airport of Buenos Aires city, Argentina (SABE).

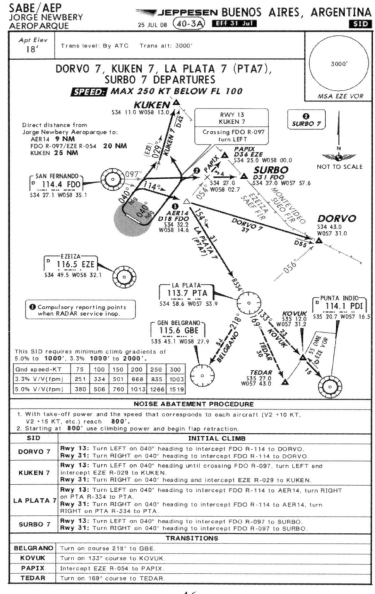

1 and 2) ICAO / IATA designation. Chart number and date of creation

3) Name of the City and Country

4) Elevation of the airport

5) Information regarding the transition level and transition altitude

6) MSA of the sector in a certain radius on a beacon

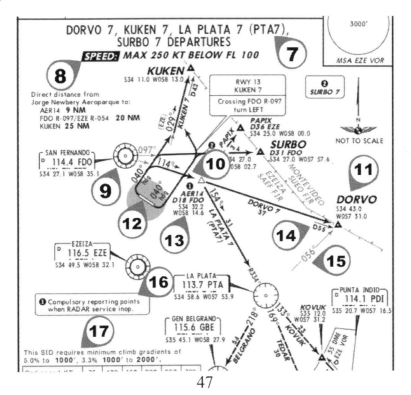

At the beginning of the aerial or graphic view, a series of names corresponding to the same SID appears. This is because the SID will be named depending on the end point through which you want to depart. For example, if the flight passes through "DORVO", the SID will be called DORVO 7. Point 8 has a speed restriction. Any information that is in a black box will be considered an operational restriction.

9) Radio reference aids for the procedure

10) Flight courses to follow to perform the procedure

11) Notification point. From this last point of the chart, the airway begins, or it is about to start

12) Representation of the aerodrome and the runway

13) Intermediate point with coordinates and additional notification represented by the black circle and the number one

14) Distance from the VOR FDO to the DORVO position

15) DORVO reference radial with respect to the VOR EZE

16) Information table on the additional notification in point 13

17) Additional requirement for this SID

Having understood the graphic symbology, let's now look at the textual description of the procedure and its limitations:

NOISE ABATEMENT PROCEDURE		
1. With take-off power and the speed that corresponds to each aircraft (V2 +10 KT, V2 +15 KT, etc.) reach **800'**. 2. Starting at **800'** use climbing power and begin flap retraction. ⓘ**18**		
SID	INITIAL CLIMB	
DORVO 7	**Rwy 13:** Turn LEFT on 040° heading to intercept FDO R... ⓘ**19** ...RVO. **Rwy 31:** Turn RIGHT on 040° heading to intercept FDO R... RVO.	
KUKEN 7	**Rwy 13:** Turn LEFT on 040° heading until crossing FDO R-0... turn LEFT and intercept EZE R-029 to KUKEN. **Rwy 31:** Turn RIGHT on 040° heading and intercept EZE R-029 to KUKEN.	
LA PLATA 7	**Rwy 13:** Turn LEFT on 040° heading to intercept FDO R-114 to AER14, turn RIGHT on PTA R-334 to PTA. **Rwy 31:** Turn RIGHT on 040° heading to intercept FDO R-114 to AER14, turn RIGHT on PTA R-334 to PTA.	
SURBO 7	**Rwy 13:** Turn LEFT on 040° heading to intercept FDO R-097 to SURBO. **Rwy 31:** Turn RIGHT on 040° heading to intercept FDO R-097 to SURBO.	
TRANSITIONS ⓘ**20**		
BELGRANO	Turn on course 218° to GBE.	
KOVUK	Turn on 133° course to KOVUK.	
PAPIX	Intercept EZE R-054 to PAPIX.	
TEDAR	Turn on 169° course to TEDAR.	

18) at this point, we will stop for a few moments to explain the fundamental purpose of a noise attenuation procedure. In airports located within cities and/or in the vicinity of them, it is a requirement that aircrafts reach a certain altitude as soon as possible in order to "attenuate" the noise pollution caused by engine noise when taking off. Note that this procedure is a requirement of departure charts and not of approach charts, because during takeoff, aircraft apply all their power and maximum noise, but during approaches, the aircraft arrive with reduced power and minimum noise.

In this particular case, the noise attenuation procedure is described in clear text and requests to take off and ascend with takeoff power until it reaches 800FT and only there to begin the power reduction for the climb. This will give the aircraft the possibility to ascend to a higher speed and then reconfigure its flight.

19) At this point we find instructions for the initial climb depending on the departure to be made and the runway to be used. For example, if we perform the SURBO 7 departure from runway 31, the description details the steps to follow to the SURBO position.

20) Finally, there is sometimes information about the final transition prior to entering an airway. If it exists, here are the additional steps to follow after you have reached the end point of the chart.

Very good! We will return to the chart and learn how to make an instrumental departure. But before that, it is of the utmost importance that the crew perform the corresponding "Briefing" of the cartography to be used. Let's see.

Briefing SID SABE

Briefings are procedures that respond to the operational safety of the flight. In a briefing, it is not only sought to understand the chart that the crew is going to make, but also that both pilots have the same departure and with the same effective date, as well as it seeks to mitigate the error by an erroneous understanding of the steps to follow. Mapping Briefings usually have a structure and a series of steps to follow. The reading of the chart will depend on the flight planning.

We will plan a takeoff from SABE runway 13 and fly to the KUKEN departure point. Let's see:

Every briefing has a logical reading order. Similar to reading a book, it must be done from top to bottom and from left to right, as seen in the following example:

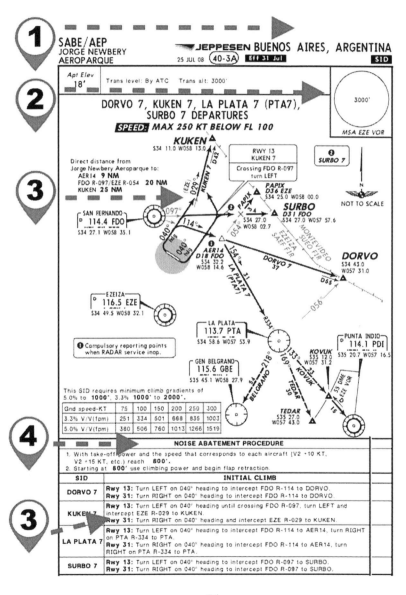

In point number one, the acronym ICAO of the airport is mentioned along with the name of the city. Subsequently, the number of the chart to confirm that both pilots have the same and then their date of preparation to verify the validity of the procedure, and as with the chart number, confirm that both pilots possess it. In point two, the elevation of the aerodrome will be mentioned, any additional information in the following table and finally the MSA for a given sector will be mentioned.

At point three, the description of the procedure begins by mentioning the name of the chart (depending on the point to be used), in our case, the chart will have the name SID KUKEN 7. After mentioning the name of the SID, we mention the speed restriction that appears in a black box and goes on to describe the procedure from the runway we are going to use and following the reference lines until we reach the end point. Note that point number three also appears at the end of the chart, in this section, we will be able to read verbatim the steps to follow during the procedure.

Finally, point four should mention the detail of the noise attenuation procedure in case the SID has one. Let's look at an example of the complete Briefing of this sid:

- "SABE, Buenos Aires, Argentina. Chart 40-3A. July 25, 2018. Elevation 18FT. Transition altitude 3000FT and MSA 3000FT over EZE VOR. SID KUKEN 7. Maximum speed 250KT below FL100. Take off from runway 13, turn left until crossing R097FDO. Then, turn left to intercept R029EZE and continue on R029EZE to position KUKEN to D42EZE. Noise abatement procedure: climb with takeoff power up to 800FT, subsequent climb power and retraction of Flaps.

Flight Operation SID (SABE)

Once the SID briefing is over, it's time to start the flight and follow the pattern indicated in the chart. SIDs are usually carried out on a continuous climb regime, but sometimes control can restrict such a regime and request a level flight leg. This does not imply that the SID should be discontinued, it only implies a change in the promotion regime.

On the other hand, in the existence of a noise attenuation procedure, the control must request any changes it wants above the minimum altitude of this procedure.

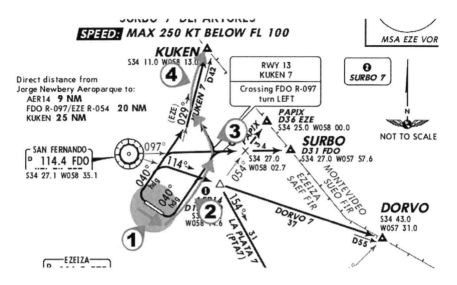

1) Take off runway 13. Runway course up to 800FT. Reduction to climb power (noise abatement procedure).

2) Turn left Heading 040° until R097FDO is intercepted.

3) Turn left Heading 360° until R029EZE is intercepted.

4) Turning to the right. Continue on R029EZE away to the KUKEN position at 42NM of EZE.

Although the procedure seems quite simple, it can gain a higher degree of complexity when different variables such as obstacles, mountain areas, adverse weather conditions, excessive volume of air traffic, radio aids out of service and other variables that we can find in the "day to day" of an air operation. In the following pages we will learn about different SIDs with different degrees of complexity.

Engine out SID (EOSID)

In addition to the traditional departure charts and their variables, there is a group of their charts for emergencies known as EOSID or "Engine Out SID". EOSIDs are designed to make an instrumental departure during an engine failure, guiding the aircraft on a safe flight path and with the minimum requirement to ascend to a safe area of operation.

Although these charts or procedures are specific to each company and made according to a specific aircraft, airports can provide, in addition, a standardized engine failure procedure for those particular aircraft or small companies that do not have such a procedure.

The purpose of EOSIDs is to take the aircraft to a safe altitude and area where the crew can carry out the checks and procedures corresponding to the failure. These areas are strategic points and free of nearby obstacles but within the vicinity of the airport so that the aircraft can return immediately if needed.

At an airport with EOSID, the crew must take off with both charts at their fingertips, that is, with the corresponding SIDs and EOSID to anticipate any contingency.

Let's look at an EOSID from Mexico Airport (MMMX).

MEXICO CITY, MEXICO
LIC BENITO JUAREZ INTL

SPECIAL ENGINE-OUT PROCEDURE

Rwys 05L/R
Allowable take-off weights for Rwys 05L/R based on a 15° banked climbing LEFT turn, commenced at D5.0 MEX VOR to a magnetic heading of 320°. Intercept and track outbound on MEX VOR R-360.

Rwys 23L/R
Allowable take-off weights for Rwys 23L/R based on a 15° banked climbing LEFT turn, commenced at D5.4 MEX VOR direct to MEX VOR. Continue climb outbound on MEX VOR R-360.

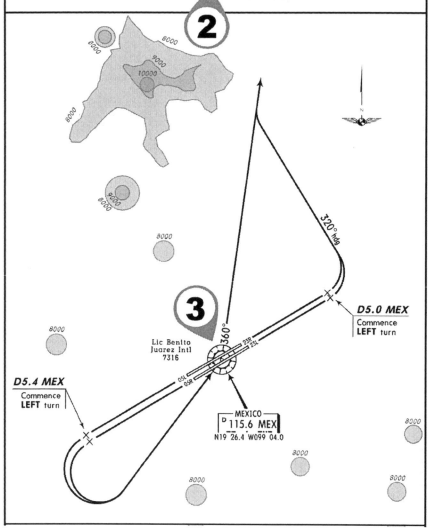

Starting with the header, point one, on your left leaves room for the logo of each airline. Followed by them and like the rest of the charts, the numbering of this chart and its date of preparation. At the end of the header, the name of the city, country and the name of the airport.

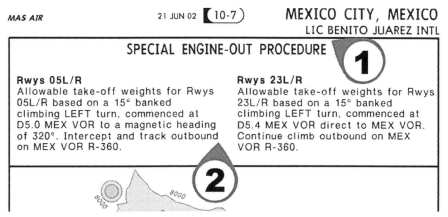

In the second section, point two, we find the title of the chart and a textual description of the procedure for the different runways.

For example, the departure procedure with engine failure for the 23L and 23R runways details: maintain runway course up to D5.4 MEX VOR, then begin a turn of no more than 15° of inclination from the left direct to MEX VOR. Then continue the climb by R360 MEX VOR away and follow the instructions of the control.

Let's see what happens taking off from runway 05R. Maintain runway heading up and off until D5.0 MEX VOR. From there and with a maximum inclination of 15°, make a turn to course 320° until you intercept R360 MEX VOR away.

Finally, the graphic description of what was detailed verbatim in the previous point. In all cases, the aircraft will end up moving away from the MEX VOR 360 radial.

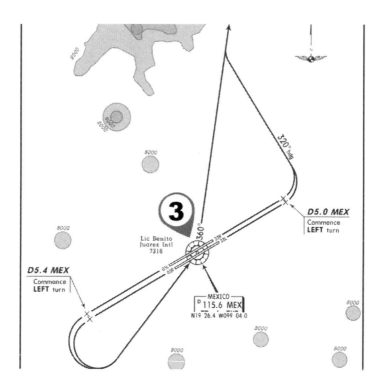

SID Overview

This type of cartography works in support of traditional SID but is considered only an informative and non-operational chart, that is, it cannot be flown. It offers an overview of the area to be flown over, obstacles, waypoints, radio aids and represents the geographical elevations. Although it is a very rare type of SID, it is very useful for the crew. Let's look at the SID OVERVIEW of Sao Paulo (SBGR):

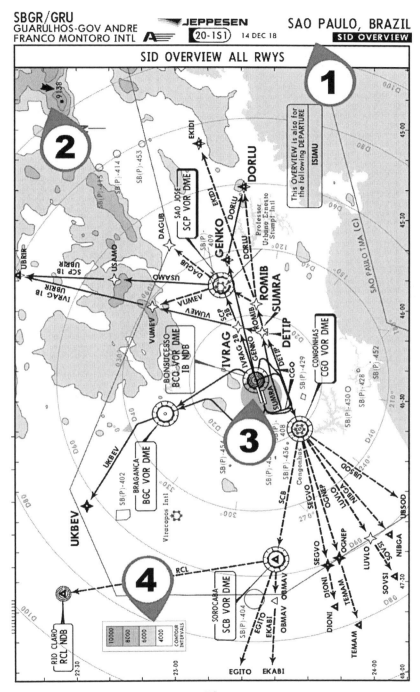

In point one we find the header, and like the rest of the chart, it provides information about the airport, chart number, date of creation and name of the city.

At point number two we see an arrow and a value corresponding to the elevation of the highest obstacle in the area.

Point number three represents the airport area and its runways along with the available beacons.

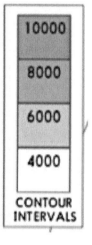

Finally, in point four we find a scale of elevations on feet with a representative color code. From the lightest to the darkest, increasing the value of the elevation. Looking at the icon in point two, we notice that its value matches the color code, which is the darkest and adopts a value of up to 10,000FT.

SID over mountains

Having understood most of the concepts applied to SID charts, let's now look at an interesting variable of these charts. Let's travel to Argentina to visit the north of the country and the city of San Salvador de Jujuy. Surrounded by mountains, it offers a rather peculiar departure procedure. Let's see:

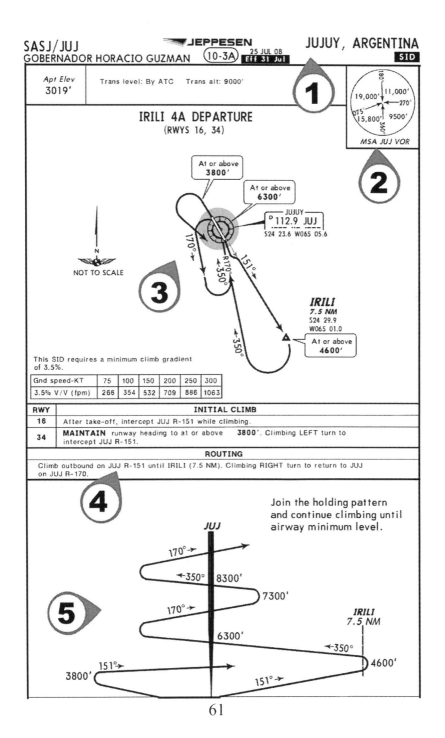

Point number one has a traditional header and is similar to the rest of the SIDs. Point number two refers to the MSA with considerable values due to the geography of the area.

Point number three represents the diagram or path that the aircraft must follow to perform this departure procedure.

In point four we find a textual description of the steps to follow to perform the procedure.

Finally, in point number five, we see how a vertical profile is added to the SID, a detail that in those previously studied did not appear or was perhaps unnecessary. In this particular scenario and due to its complex geography, aircraft must perform the departure procedure according to the diagram and at the same time make an uphill wait in order to overcome all possible obstacles that the geography of the area may present to them.

Let's now travel to the city of Bogotá in Colombia and get to know another instrumental starting chart with the same consideration as Jujuy's chart. A mountainous area that has an uphill departure procedure to overcome all the obstacles in the area and reach the airway safely and efficiently. Let's see:

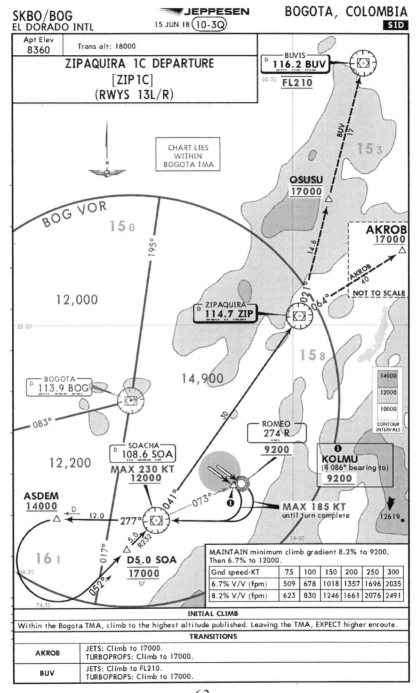

This SID begins with a traditional header informing the ICAO/IATA code of the airport, the date of creation of the charter and its respective number, the city and the country. In the next section, we find the elevation of the airport, the transition altitude and in a box, the proper name of the chart indicating that it applies to runways 13L and 13R.

After the descriptive diagram, in the lower right margin, we find a box on the requirement of the minimum climb gradient that the aircraft must meet in this area. Just below this box are the descriptive rows of the procedure, the initial climb, a common step for both transitions and then the description of each of them.

Before analyzing the operation of this chart, YOUR TURN again! Observing the entire chart and considering that the MSA of the sector is not reported:

- What is the elevation of the highest obstacle in the area?

Note that in each of the points to fly over the chart, restrictions are detailed, both of minimum speed and minimum altitudes to be met.

Let's go into detail about the procedure and try to get to the AKROB position!

After takeoff, the aircraft must fly directly to the NDB R, after passing through R, direct right turn to the VOR SOA, in continuous climb and with a speed restriction of 185KT until the turn is finished. After passing through VOR SOA, direct to the ASDEM position by R277SOA until 12.0NM and up to 14000FT. Subsequent ASDEM, shift on the left towards VOR SOA again entering through R232SOA and ascending to 17000FT at least 5.0NM of SOA. Afterwards, direct to SOA. Next step, fly directly to VOR ZIP, course 041° at 30.0NM maintaining at least 17000 FT. When you reach the VOR ZIP, turn right directly to the AKROB position on R064ZIP at 40.0NM.

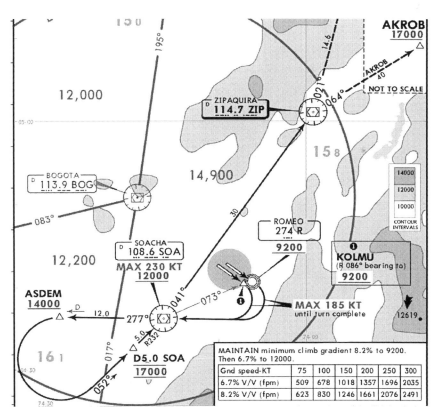

Remember that the SID charts are diagrammed to maximize the flow of traffic in the area, however, air traffic control may request that the aircraft depart from the SID procedure for a few moments or permanently. If this happens, it is the obligation of the crew to comply with the control instructions as long as it does not affect the safety of the flight. In each diagram, the minimum altitudes to be flown over outside the SID procedure are presented.

Observing this SID of Bogotá, we note that outside the planned route of the procedure, there are minimum flight altitudes, for example, north of the VOR BOG 12,000FT and to the east of 14,900FT. Both altitudes are outside the color scale provided by the chart but are of great consideration at the time of mating the procedure.

Chapter 3

Route charts. Airways (AWY)

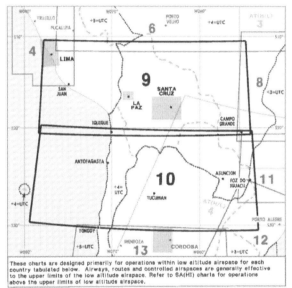

Routes charts

Introduction

Once the SID has been abandoned, it is time to start the route en route, still on the rise and already on the cruise section. Route charts do not differ much from traditional maps of car routes, where there are routes or paths of one or two directions, with a name and a distance between two points, adding a route symbology specific to each chart. The same thing happens on air routes, there is a path or route that connects two points, a distance between them and an aeronautical symbology that describes the most relevant details to be known.

Like the previous charts, route charts have a traditional format and have an information structure that allows a correct order of reading. Although this structure may be modified by some data, it usually maintains the following format:

Header	
Diagram	
Changes	
Air space	Diagram
Communications	
Notes	
FL	

Let's look at an example of a complete chart. The following image represents the left section of the previous format:

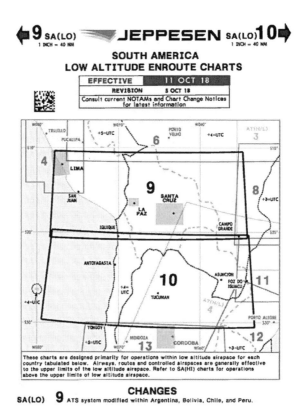

Cartographic Symbology

Let's start by analyzing a traditional header. In the same way as the previous chart, the header provides the first information to read:

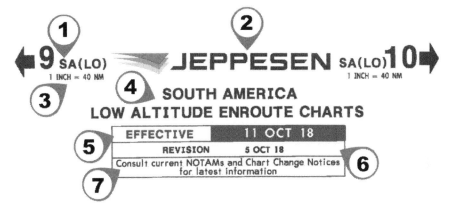

1) In this first point, we find the number of the chart and its name. In this case, we read chart number 9 SA (South America) of low altitude or LO (low). Note that to the right of the header there is another chart number with an arrow to the right. This is because the roadmaps are made on both sides, that is, printed on both sides and each side for a different region. If the pilot opens the chart to the left, he will read the information for zone 9 and if he does so to the right he will read the information for zone number 10. The geographical space covered by each of these areas is described in the following section or "Coverage Diagram".

2) Manufacturer's logo. As we mentioned at the beginning of this manual, we will base the analysis of cartography on JEPPESEN publications, a world leader in aeronautical cartographic publications

3) At this point we find the scale of the graphic representation.

4) Coverage area of both charts (zone 9 and zone 10).

5 and 6) Day of the effectiveness of the chart after the last revision according to point 6.

7) Additional information about special changes or alerts.

Now let's look at the coverage diagram of our chart to better understand point 1 of the heading:

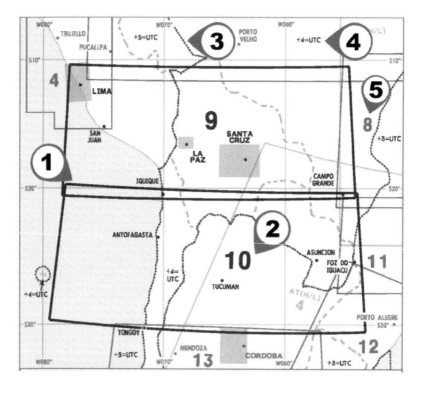

1) This first point represents the two coverage areas of the chart. Section number 9 covers Bolivia, part of Peru and part of Brazil. Section number 10 covers northern Argentina, part of Paraguay, Chile and southern Bolivia.

2) Chart number according to header.

3) Line of border limits between countries.

4) Time difference with respect to local time.

5) Number of charts from other areas not covered by this chart.

Finally, we arrive at the additional information section where we will find notes regarding special instructions and a table of cruise levels by sector.

TRANSPONDER SETTINGS
(SECONDARY SURVEILLANCE RADAR - SSR)
FOR BEACON CODE PROCEDURES SEE ENROUTE PAGE SA-17 AND CONSECUTIVE PAGES.

ALTIMETER SETTING
USE QNE (STANDARD ALTIMETER SETTING)
EXCEPTION: USE QNH (LOCAL STATION PRESSURE) FOR-
TAKE-OFF AND CLIMB UNTIL PASSING TRANSITION ALTITUDE.
DESCENT AND LANDING AS SOON AS PASSING TRANSITION LEVEL.
TRANSITION ALTITUDES/LEVELS ARE SHOWN ON APPROACH CHARTS
AND/OR MAY BE REQUESTED FROM ATC.

CRUISING ALTITUDES

(VFR ADD 500')
EXCEPTIONS
BARRANQUILLA, BOGOTA FIRs
VFR prohibited SS-SR.
LIMA FIR
VFR cruising altitudes same as IFR.

Having understood the initial section of the chart, it is time to open it on one of the two sides, if we do it for the left we will read chart number 9 and if we do it for the right, we will read chart number 10. Let's read the latter, but first, let's remember the area that our chart will cover:

- Northern Argentina (Tucumán and area)

- Northern Chile (Antofagasta and area)

- Central and Southern Paraguay (Assumption and area)

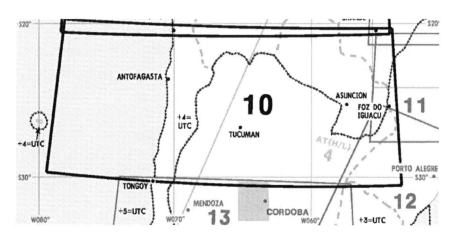

Let's take an excerpt from this chart to analyse its different sections and symbols. Considering that there are a huge number of representations and symbols, we will try to learn the most relevant ones. Let's look at the following excerpt from the chart without reference numbers to avoid covering symbols and then we will analyse it in sections:

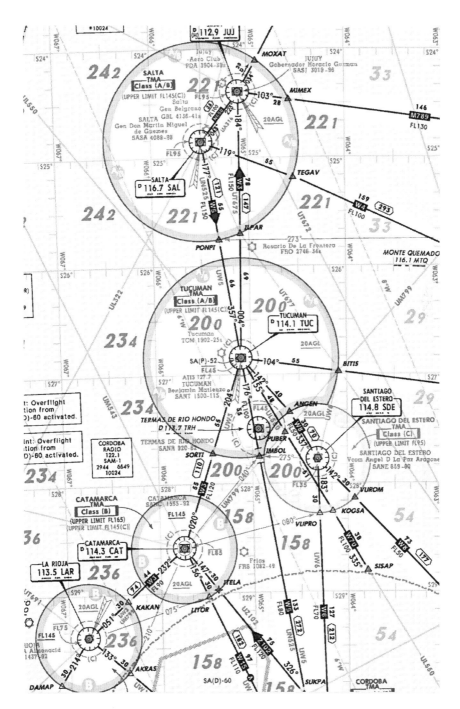

To achieve a better visualization, we will take parts of this chart and get to know its different symbols and sections. Let's start with the North zone:

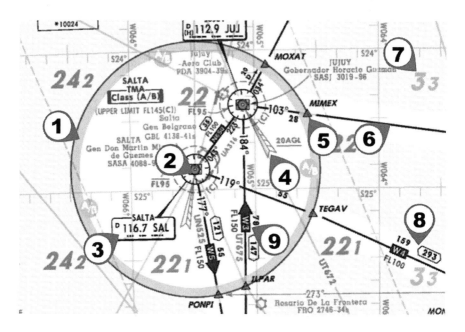

1) The circles surrounding the airport area represent the TMA of the place. Its radius may vary, and may even be attached to a TMA from another place.

2 and 3) Graphic representation of the airport and its radio aids.

4) ILS command prompt, in case the airport has a system installed.

5) A black triangle represents a mandatory notification point and a white triangle represents a non-mandatory notification point.

6) The black strokes represent the routes or airways.

7) the numbers outside the TMA areas or sections of the airways, represent the minimum safety altitudes outside the route. They are represented with 2 or 3 numbers, the large number represents the altitude of a thousand feet and the small number complements the information with hundreds of feet. In this example, the minimum off-route safety altitude is 3300FT. On the other hand, to the west of the chart, the minimum off-route latitude is 24200FT.

8) A number within a box reports the total distance from a mandatory reporting point to another of the same nature.

9) Symbol of the airway and details of it. As we mentioned earlier, the airways can be one- or two-way. This information is represented with a black arrow and the name of the airway when it is a one-way route, or with a black square with the same information when it comes to a two-way route. In our case, it is a one-way route with the name of W3. Above the arrow we find a number that represents the distance between the previous and the next point. Just below the arrow represents the minimum flight level for that airway, in this case FL150. To the right of the arrow, we find information about an upper airway in the same direction as the W3, it is the UT675 airway, but for it no information is provided in this chart.

Continuing with the chart, let's look at another section and try to identify the points learned. YOUR TURN!

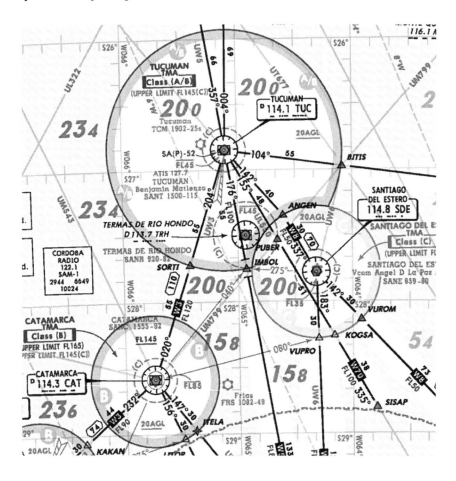

- What is the distance between Catamarca airport and Tucumán?
- Is the route that unites them one-way or a two-way one?
- Which of these two airports has an ILS system?
- What is the minimum off-route altitude to the east of Catamarca?
- What is the minimum FL of the W3 airway?

Terminal Area Charts

As we mentioned earlier, TMA zones are represented with a large circle that can vary their radius but always concerns an airport. In areas where the TMA is more complex and extensive, it can cover several airports. For this reason, there are roadmaps, specific to the TMA and are known as "Area Charts". Let's look at some examples starting with the area charter of the City of Buenos Aires, Argentina. Here the TMA BAIRES is represented:

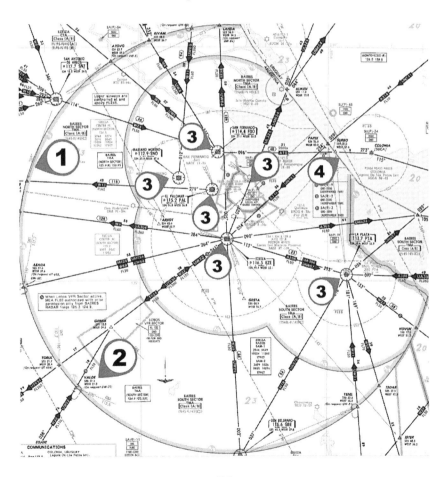

1) The largest circle represents the coverage area of the chart or TMA of the area. In this case, it involves six airports.

2) Points of entry and departure of the TMA

3) Airports involved within the TMA

4) Border boundary between Argentina and Uruguay

Let's take a closer look at this menu and learn some additional details. YOUR TURN AGAIN!

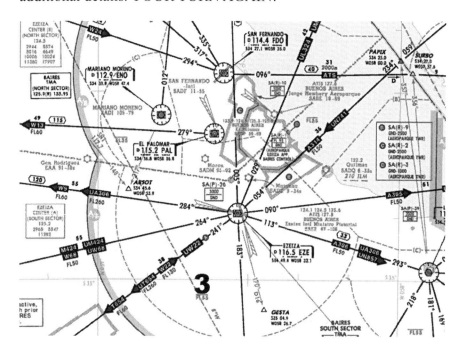

- *Can you identify which airports have an ILS system and which do not?*

Let's look at another example of area charts. Let's go to Quito, Ecuador:

Unlike the previous area chart, geographical considerations typical of the area are represented in Quito. An area with fewer airports within the same TMA.

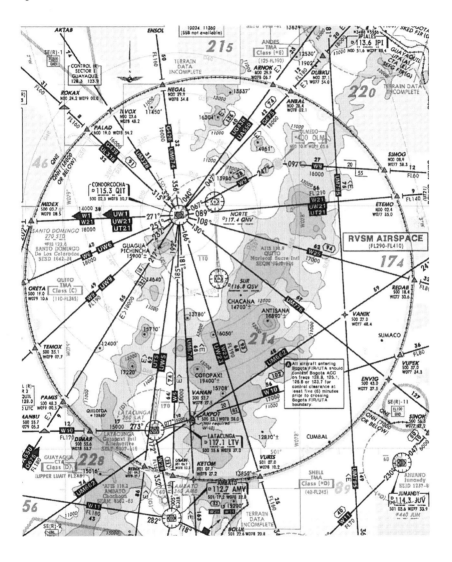

Let's look at an excerpt from this chart and analyze its details:

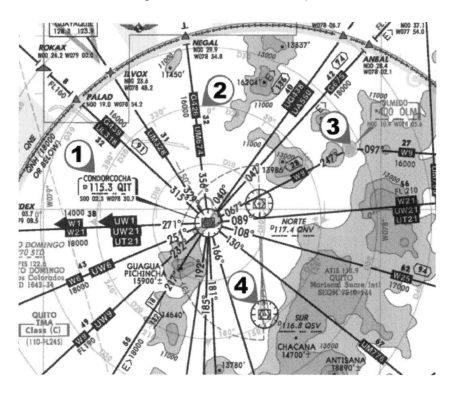

1) Information about the main radio help of Quito airport
2) Two-way aircraft
3) NDB as an additional reference to navigation
4) Additional VOR station related to the approach charts

      Having understood the main concepts of the route charts, let's move on to practice and analyze a real flight situation by planning according to the parameters offered by the chart.

Practical Analysis I

Let's plan an international flight from Ezeiza International Airport, Buenos Aires, Argentina (SAEZ) to Montevideo International Airport, Uruguay (SUMU). To do this, we will use the following route map:

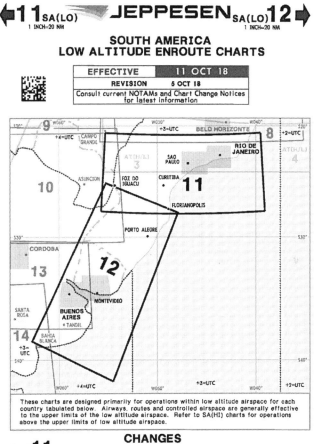

- What chart number should we take to analyze our route?. The number 11 or the number 12?

If your answer was chart number 12, it's CORRECT! Let's open chart number 12 and see the route:

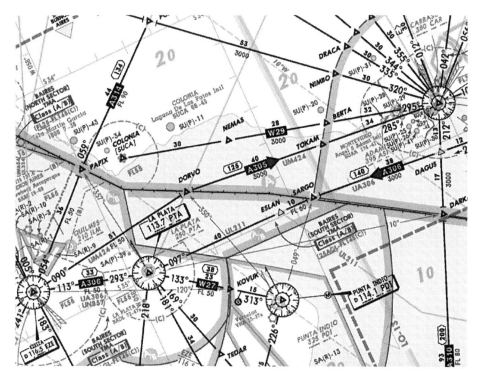

Let's take a moment to analyze our chart. We must obtain the following information:Let's take a moment to analyze our chart. We must obtain the following information:

- *Course*
- *Notification Points*
- *Total Distance*
- *Airway*
- *Minimum FL*

Try to obtain this data before moving on to the next page and then we will analyze it together.

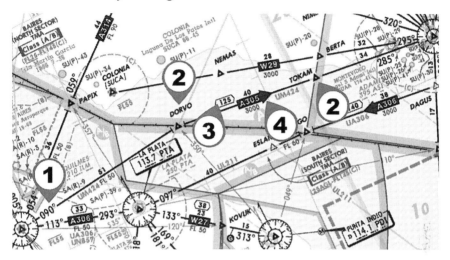

Analyzing the roadmap, we find that the initial course is 090° from the VOR EZE (point 1), 51NM to the first DORVO notification point (point 2). From there we continue along the A305 airway with a minimum altitude of 3000FT (point 4), 40 NM to the next TOKAM point (point 2). Finally, we continue 34NM directly to Montevideo airport, having traveled a total of 125NM (point 3).

If your answers from the previous page match this description, you have achieved it!

Now, let's see what happens on the return flight from Montevideo airport to Ezeiza Airport. You will be alone here but you have already equipped yourself with the necessary tools to solve this situation. The goal will be to obtain the same data that we have obtained on the outbound flight, but now in the return section. Let's take a look at the chart again:

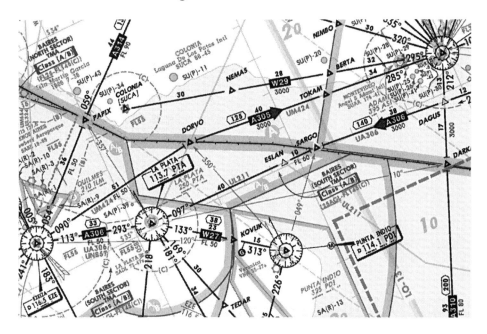

Practical Analysis II

Let's change the scenery and go to the Caribbean. Let's analyze the following chart and obtain the necessary data to fly from the city of Barranquilla, Colombia to the city of Maracaibo, Venezuela. An international flight in which you will have to make the right decisions about the routes to choose and their different sections. Remember that the essential data are:

- *Course*
- *Notification Points*
- *Total Distance*
- *Airway and Minimum FL*

Here is your enroute chart. In the first instance, you must select the chart number to use depending on the area to fly over.

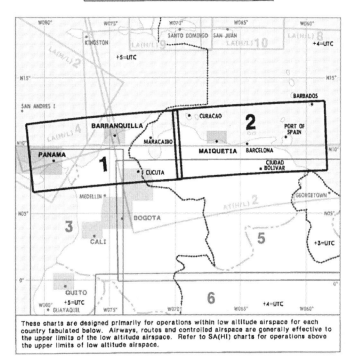

YOUR TURN! Open the chart in the correct number and get the data!

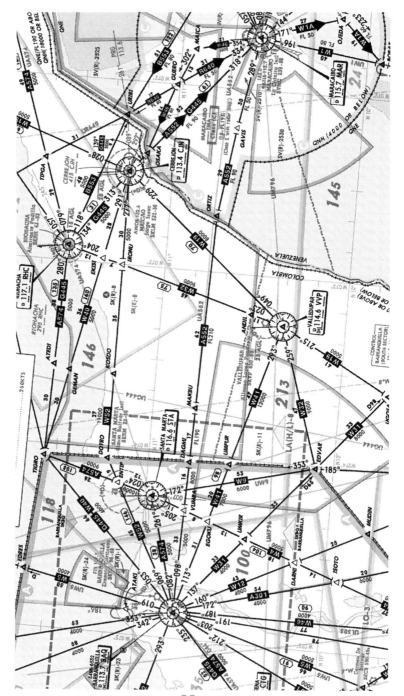

I assume that you have managed to obtain the necessary data for the flight from Barranquilla to Maracaibo. Anyway, and as a check, we are going to analyze the chart together.

Analyzing the chart we see that the correct airway is the A552 with an initial course from VOR BAQ of 098° to the first VUMBA point at 33NM of BAQ, then 16 NM more until DAGMI and later an additional 17 NM to MAKBU. While we note that the altitudes and minimum FL up to MAKBU are growing, the right thing to do is to adopt the minimum FL of the A552 airway that indicates a value of FL210. After MAKBU, the airway continues 62NM to the OTIZ position, a border point and entry point to the area of control of Venezuela.

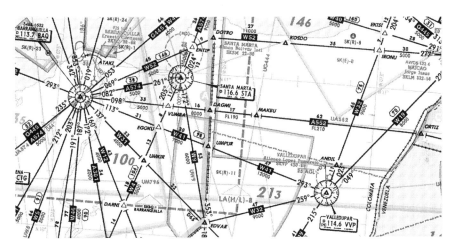

Although as we have learned before, white triangles are non-mandatory notification points and black triangles are mandatory notification points, as long as it is a point in a border area, the current control will end the communication and transfer the flight to the control of the next country.

Once entering Venezuelan territory, after the ORTIZ notification point, the flight must continue for 29NM to the GAVIS position. Note that since ORTIZ the minimum FL of the A552 airway has decreased to FL090 and later GAVIS to FL050.

Finally, from GAVIS we continue for 30NM directly to Maracaibo, descending to the FL indicated on the airway or already from GAVIS, the flight could continue under the precise instructions of the control.

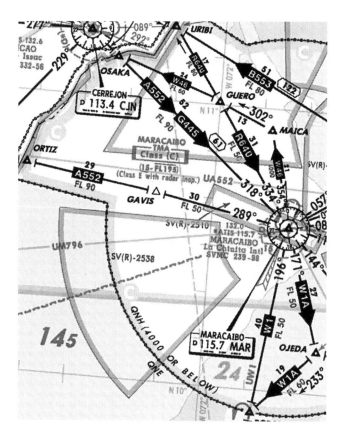

Well done! You have arrived in Maracaibo!

CHAPTER 4

Standard Terminal Arrival Route (STAR)

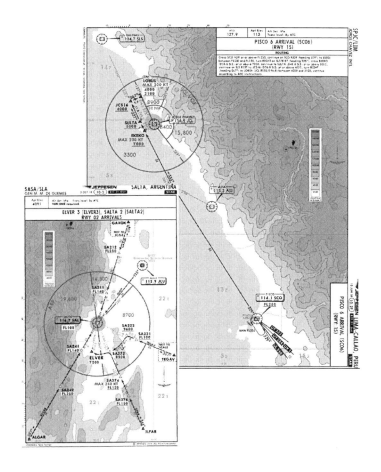

Arrivals
charts

General information

Similar to departure charts (SIDs), STARs represent a diagram of the area where the aircraft would operate if you want to use a standardized income. Like SID charts, STAR charts have a format divided into different sections. This format can be presented both vertically and horizontally depending on the information. Let's see:

The header respects the same format as the previous charts. The aerial view has similar characteristics but with additional information such as the MSA. The lower section is composed of information related to the descent and information on the points to follow until reaching the final level. This final section can be omitted depending on the airport and format of the chart.

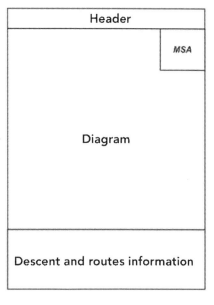

This chart format is flexible concerning the position of the information, and its location may vary in different dialog boxes. Let's start with the analysis of a simple STAR (Barcelona, LEBL) and continue with a slightly more complete one (Buenos Aires, SABE):

Analysis and Symbology Barcelona (LEBL)

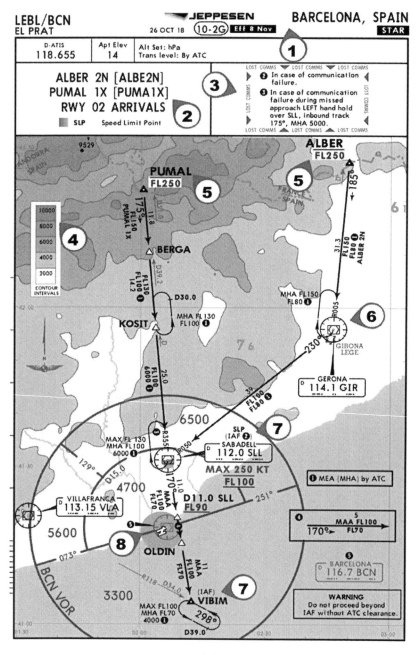

1) The header responds to the same format as the SID chart, starting from left to right, ICAO/IATA designation of the airport, chart number and date of preparation, city and country.

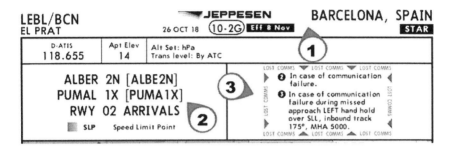

2) Point two also maintains the same format by naming the chart depending on the starting point of the chart.

3) In point three we find a clarification in clear text of the steps to follow in case of communication failure.

4) Here again we find a terrain elevation scale, where the darkest tones respond to higher elevations and vice versa.

5) Starting points of the procedure for entering the terminal.

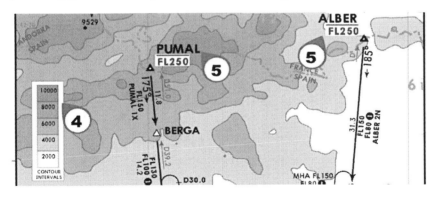

6) Section of change of course to the terminal with a non-mandatory published waiting procedure, except for requirements of the ATC or the crew's own.

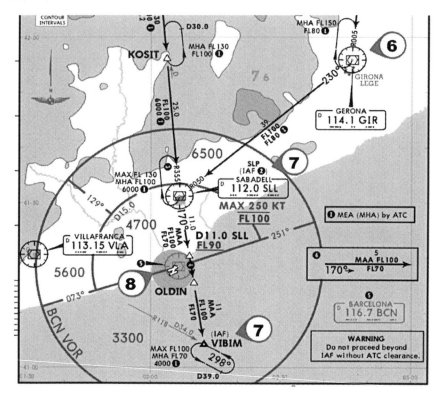

7) These two points are known as IAF (Initial Approach Fix) and are the end point of the STAR, right where the approach procedure begins.

8) Graphic representation of the airport and its runways.

Note that there are dialog boxes in the right margin of the chart, where restrictions are clarified at certain points of the procedure.

Operation in Barcelona (LEBL)

Now let's see how to fly a STAR. Let's analyse how the route of the plane should be until we reach the IAF.

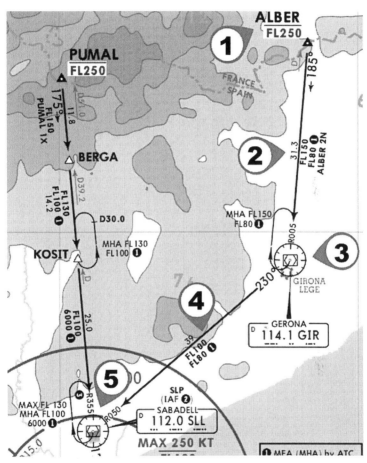

For our example, the STAR starts in ALBER to FL250, from there, course 185° 31.3NM in descent to FL150 to GIR where there is the possibility of waiting on R005GIR. After GIR, turn right to course 230° 39NM, descending to FL100 until reaching the IAF over SLL VOR.

Analysis and Symbology Buenos Aires (SABE)

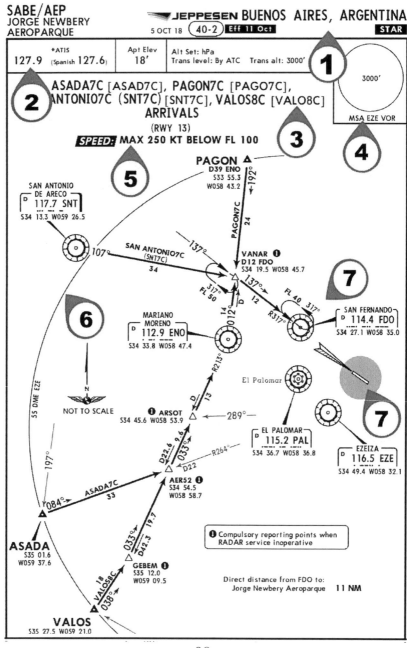

Looking at SABE's STAR, we see that the header respects the traditional information format. In the second information section we find the frequencies of the ATIS, the elevation of the airport and information related to the transition altitude.

Point number three represents as many names as possible for this chart. In the same way as SIDs, the name of the chart will be given to you by the starting point of the procedure. For example, if the plane starts the STAR at the ASADA point, this chart will be called ASADA7C.

In point four, and unlike the Barcelona charter, here we find information about the MSA about the VOR EZE. Points five and six represent operational limitations. On the one hand, a speed restriction of 250KT below FL100 is reported and on the other hand, the limits of the terminal control zone or TMA represented with an arc of 55NM of the VOR EZE are plotted.

Finally, we arrive at the end point of the STAR, the VOR FDO, but the final approach to the airport of Buenos Aires, Argentina (SABE). From here, the flight will continue with the approach procedure that the crew wishes to perform.

Having understood its most important points, it is time to fly our STAR and get to the IAF of the approach to the SABE airport. Our starting point will be the ROAST position and we will have to get to the VOR FDO.

Operation in Buenos Aires (SABE)

Now let's see how to operate the SABE STAR. Let's analyse how the route of the plane should be until we reach the IAF.

We start from the ROAST position, the entrance to the terminal. From there, course 084° 33NM to position AER52. At this point, there is a clarification where it indicates that in the event of the failure of the radar control, this point becomes a mandatory notification point. After AER52, turn left course 033° 9.6NM to the ARSOT position (located on R289EZE). Later, in the same course, 13NM until you reach the ENO VOR.

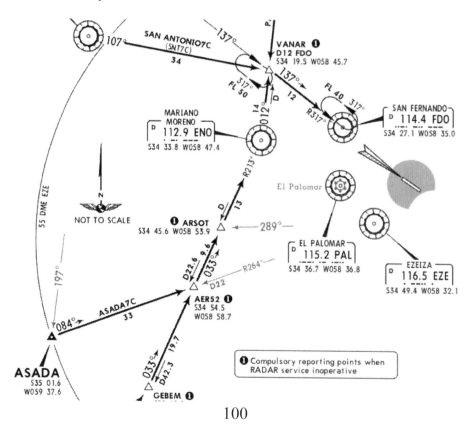

Posterior ENO VOR, left turn, course 012°, 14NM to the VANAR position where there is a standby procedure with a minimum flight level of FL050. Finally, from the VANAR position (R317FDO) and after completing the waiting procedure, continue to FDO VOR in progress 137° 12NM. Upon arrival at FDO VOR, there is another waiting procedure, before starting the approach procedure in use for SABE.

So far we have known the variables of the STAR charts. Each of them can present different formats in the information provided. Considering that the geography of our planet is extremely variable, in mountainous areas we will surely find charts with a less traditional format than those that we can find in flat areas or near the ocean. This is represented in the two previous charts, where the Barcelona chart represents the elevations of the terrain with a color code and in the Buenos Aires chart this information is omitted since it is located on the plain above the Atlantic Ocean.

Analysis of Salta, Argentina (SASA)

Let's now look at another example of a mountainous area where the flight path could be affected, the situation is contemplated in the STAR format. The city of Salta, Argentina, is surrounded by mountainous areas. To the west by the Andes mountain range and to the east by small geographical elevations. This makes Salta airport a complex place for the realization of the STAR. Let's know your details:

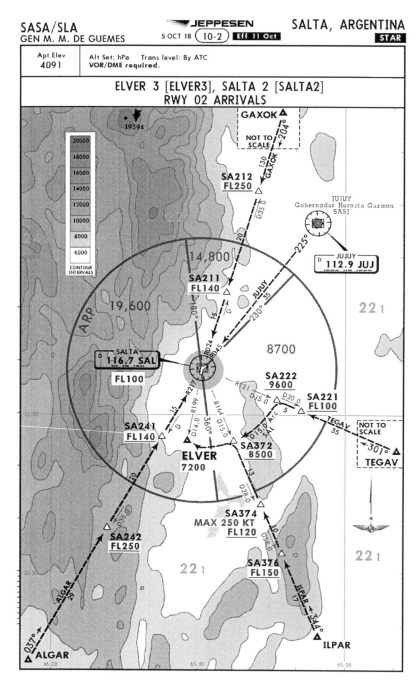

Unlike the previous chart, Salta's chart presents a restriction on the equipment of the aircraft, which could prevent the procedure from being carried out. Let's look at the header and the information section. YOUR TURN!

What do you think the restriction is?

We will see the correct answer on the next pages, so you will have some time to look at the chart and find the solution. Continuing, we observe that the header has a traditional format. Then the information section reports the considerable elevation of the airport and below, the possible names of this STAR.

Like the Barcelona charter, this STAR has a chromatic scale of elevations over the west of the airport, a mountain range area. The darker tones indicate greater elevation and vice versa.

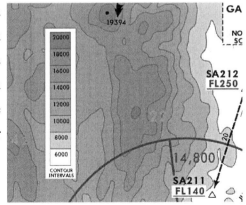

Returning to the question on the previous page, the answer is highlighted in darker chart ("bold" style). The information section indicates; "VOR/DME required" informing you of the obligation to have this equipment to make this chart.

Other special considerations of this chart can be found on the flight route from the ILPAR position to the ELVER position, where at each point to fly over there are FL restrictions and minimum altitudes to be crossed. These restrictions are due to the different elevations of the terrain on the flight path during the descent and to the ELVER end point. Let's look at these items in the chart and proceed to the procedure:

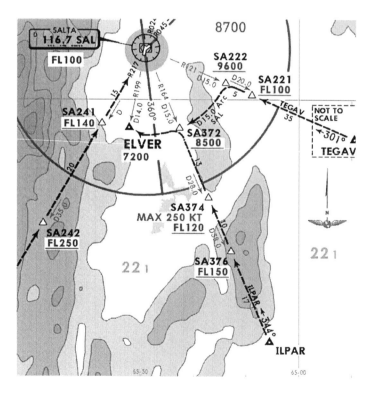

Operation in Salta, Argentina (SASA)

As an example, imagine that our flight comes from Sector South and at the time of reaching the ILPAR position, it is downhill crossing FL200. From ILPAR continues with course 344°, 17NM to point SA376 where there is a restriction of FL150. Subsequently, we continue with the same course 344°, 10 NM to position SA374 and here there are two restrictions, one of speed (MAX 250KT) and the other of FL120. In compliance with this, the next step will be to reach position SA372 with a restriction of 8500FT. From there, start an ARCO DME of 15NM to the ELVER position (IAF) in descent to 7200FT and then continue with the approach chart for runway 02.

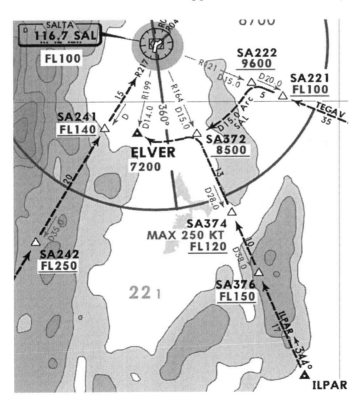

Overview STAR (SBGR)

Like the SID charts, we also find the complementary charts to the traditional STAR charts, the STAR Overview.

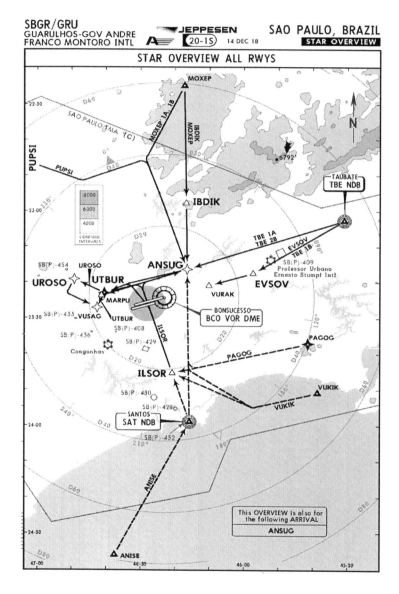

STAR overviews fulfill the same function as SID overviews, helping the mapping of entry or departure from an area control area where different points of initiation or end of the procedure can be found. Let's consider the overview as a global map of the area to fly over, and as such, it will provide information on the most relevant points in the area. Let's remember that Overviews are not operational charts, but informative, that is, they do not meet the necessary parameters to be "flying" with the aircraft.

Airport Familiarization (SBRG)

Continuing with the airport of the city of Sao Paulo, Brazil, there are a series of charts that help you familiarize yourself with the airport and its geography through representative graphs. In the same way as Overviews, these charts are not operational but fulfill the role of being informative charts, so they do not consist of operating procedures.

Airport familiarization charts are used by the crew during the cruise stage to know the place they will have to approach, their geography, their considerations and a panoramic view of the run(s). A type of extremely useful cartography that offers the possibility of knowing the area through a graphic and photographic description. Let's get to know this chart, in addition to the STAR, which will allow us to familiarize ourselves with the airport of Sao Paulo, Brazil (SBGR):

SBGR/GRU
GUARULHOS-GOV ANDRE 28 DEC 18 (29-01)
FRANCO MONTORO INTL

JEPPESEN — AIRPORT FAMILIARIZATION

SAO PAULO, BRAZIL

1. High Terrain Directly North and West of Airport
2. Low Visibility Operating Procedures at Airport
3. Numerous Prohibited and Restricted Areas Near Airport

Apt. Elev	**2461'**
11 NM Northeast Sao Paulo	
S23 26.1 W046 28.4	

MSA BCO VOR: 7000' / 6000'

OVERVIEW

1) Traditional header format with information related to the airport, the charter and the city
2) Information section on procedures, areas and geography of the ground
3) Elevation of the aerodrome. Its location with respect to the city and its geographical coordinates
4) MSA of the sector on BCO VOR
5) Panoramic photograph of the airport and area
6) Diagram on the map of the airport and area
7) View of panoramic photography with respect to the airport

Operation in México (MMMX)

Continuing with the traditional STAR format, let's go from Sao Paulo airport to Mexico City airport.

One of the STARs at MMMX airport has a peculiarity with respect to the STAR seen so far. In this case, the chart starts from the airport itself and moves away from it to leave the aircraft in a different sector and from there to be able to start the approach procedure to the airport.

Like SID charts, this MMMX STAR offers a textual description of the procedure in order to collaborate in the graphic understanding of the chart. Let's look at the complete chart and then analyze its different sections:

MMMX/MEX	JEPPESEN	MEXICO CITY, MEXICO
BENITO JUAREZ INTL	17 NOV 17 (10-2E)	STAR

D-ATIS	Apt Elev	
127.65	7316	Alt Set: IN (MB on req) Trans level: FL195

MEXICO 3B (MEX3B) ARRIVAL
(RWYS 23L/R)

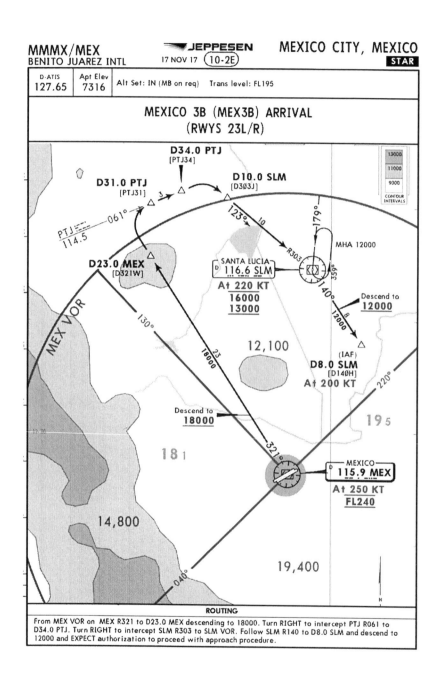

ROUTING
From MEX VOR on MEX R321 to D23.0 MEX descending to 18000. Turn RIGHT to intercept PTJ R061 to D34.0 PTJ. Turn RIGHT to intercept SLM R303 to SLM VOR. Follow SLM R140 to D8.0 SLM and descend to 12000 and EXPECT authorization to proceed with approach procedure.

Start with an informative header. From left to right, the name of the airport, the ICAO/IATA designation, the date of preparation and the chart number and the name of the city.

MMMX/MEX BENITO JUAREZ INTL	JEPPESEN 17 NOV 17 (10-2E)	MEXICO CITY, MEXICO STAR
D-ATIS 127.65	Apt Elev 7316	Alt Set: IN (MB on req) Trans level: FL195

MEXICO 3B (MEX3B) ARRIVAL (RWYS 23L/R)

In the second section, we find the frequency of Atis, the elevation of the aerodrome and information related to the transition. Finally, in the third section, the name of the chart indicating that it can be used for both runway 23L and runway 23R. Now let's move on to the graphic view.

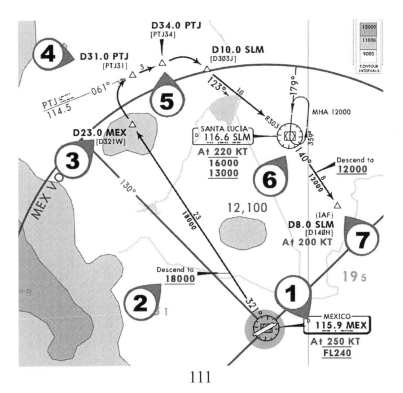

Point number one indicates the beginning of the procedure, which, unlike the rest, it starts from the vertical of the VOR MEX. After flying over the VOR, point two indicates a deviation with a descent established as a restriction to point number three to D23.0 NM. From there a turn by R061PTJ until passing point five and then another turn to SLM VOR by R303 where we find a waiting procedure at point six with two restrictions, one of speed and one of altitude. Finally, point seven, the descent to 12000FT moving away by R140SLM to the IAF to D8.0 SLM. Finally, the description of the route or "Routing". Let's see:

ROUTING
From MEX VOR on MEX R321 to D23.0 MEX descending to 18000. Turn RIGHT to intercept PTJ R061 to D34.0 PTJ. Turn RIGHT to intercept SLM R303 to SLM VOR. Follow SLM R140 to D8.0 SLM and descend to 12000 and EXPECT authorization to proceed with approach procedure.

Operation in Lima, Perú (SPJC)

Let's continue our journey through America and go to the city of Lima, Peru. There we will find an entry procedure that will place us directly in the final section of the approach to runway 15 of the airport. A STAR with various restrictions and with the particularity of being a common procedure for entry from several airways or sectors. They all converge to the same starting point and from there they will start their way to the end of runway 15.

Let's pay special attention to the restrictions on the descent in this STAR and approach Lima airport. Let's see:

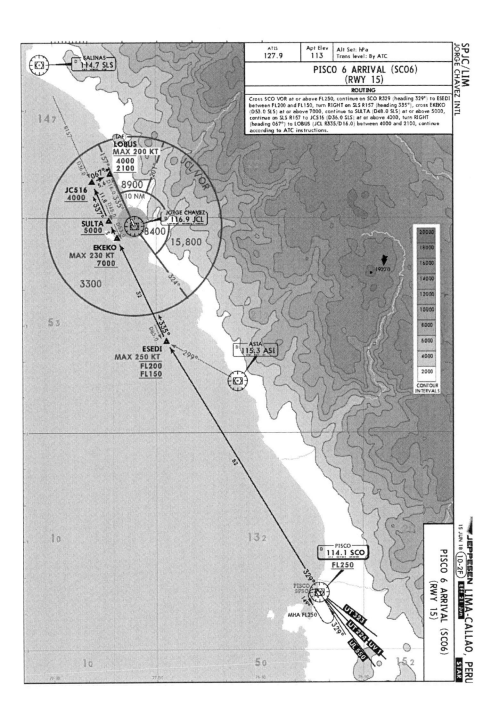

A particular chart that is presented in horizontal format with a traditional header. With an information box, we warn that the procedure begins at PISCO, a place that gives the chart its name.

ATIS 127.9	Apt Elev 113	Alt Set: hPa Trans level: By ATC
PISCO 6 ARRIVAL (SCO6)		
(RWY 15)		
ROUTING		
Cross SCO VOR at or above FL250, continue on SCO R329 (heading 329°) to ESEDI between FL200 and FL150, turn RIGHT on SLS R157 (heading 335°), cross EKEKO (D53.0 SLS) at or above 7000, continue to SULTA (D48.0 SLS) at or above 5000, continue on SLS R157 to JC516 (D36.0 SLS) at or above 4000, turn RIGHT (heading 067°) to LOBUS (JCL R335/D16.0) between 4000 and 2100, continue according to ATC instructions.		

This procedure offers the possibility of reading the "Routing" in the main section of the chart in order to assimilate its description in the first instance. Followed by this, the graphic representation. Note that the PISCO point is a common point for several airways from the southern sector. Now, let's describe the step-by-step procedure:

In the first instance, we arrived at PISCO and found a waiting procedure on R149 SCO on the left and a restriction on FL250. From there, all aircraft must follow the same transit pattern. Move away by R329SCO, 82NM to the ESEDI position where there is a MAX 250Kt speed restriction and an altitude restriction between FL200 and FL150.

Let's expand the image of this chart a little more and continue from there:

From the ESEDI position, our flight continues with a course of 355° by 32NM more to the EKEKO position where there is a speed restriction of 230KT and an altitude of 7000FT. Posterior 5NM towards SULTA in decline to 5000FT. The subsequent change of course to 337°, 11.8NM in descent to 4000FT to position JC516. Then, similar to a basic section of a circuit, turn to course 067° towards the LOBUS position where we find a speed restriction of MAX 200KT and an altitude restriction of between 4000FT and 2100FT.

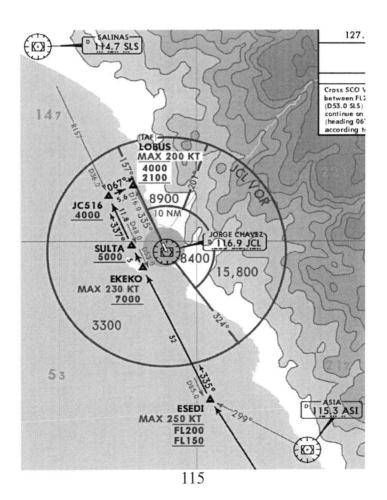

Once the LOBUS position has been reached, we have finished with the entry procedure and it has placed us right in the IAF of the approach chart for runway 15.

Note that within the area of operation of this STAR a circle on the VOR JCL is represented and reports different MSAs according to the sector to be operated.

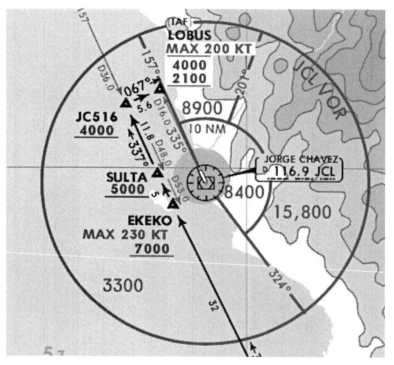

YOUR TURN AGAIN! Try to perform the correct procedures by detailing the steps to follow in the following entry chart.

Remember that analysing the procedure step by step, as we have done so far, will be the best way for you to successfully complete it! Let's see:

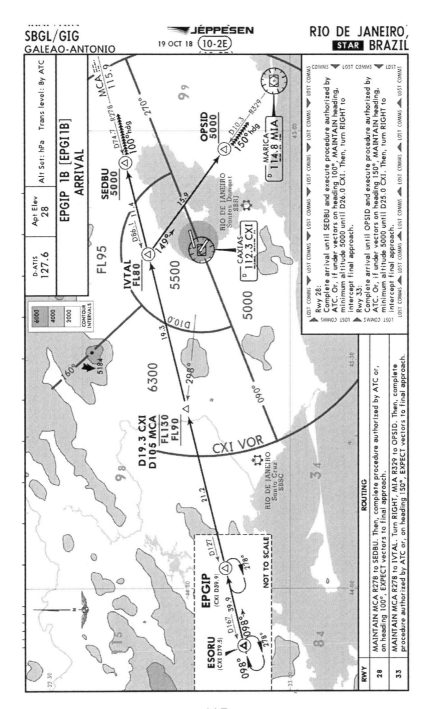

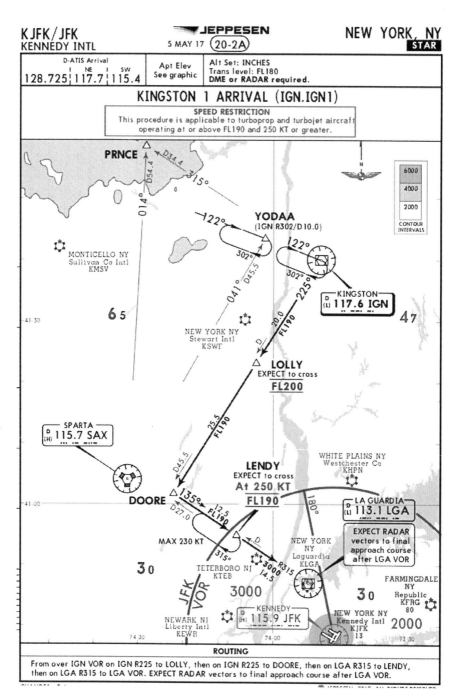

CHAPTER 5

Instrumental Approach Charts (IAC)

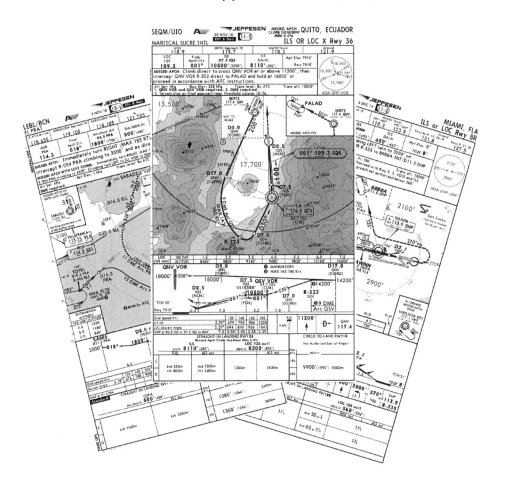

Approach charts

General information

Having reached the most relevant type of cartography for the pilot, we will take a few moments to clarify a fundamental concept before starting the study and analysis of each type of approach chart.

Instrumental approach charts are divided into two large groups and are defined according to their accuracy to perform the procedure. This precision is defined by the equipment of the aircraft, by the qualification of the pilots and by the certification of the airport where it is planned to approach.

On the one hand, we find the "non-precision" approaches known as NPA (Non- precisionApproach). A group of charts intended to guide the aircraft in its horizontal navigation to a minimum altitude and distance from the runway. In some cases, you can add assistance for vertical navigation but always within the established minimums. This type of mapping is based on the use of basic radio aids such as: VOR, NDB and ILS (only in its LOCATOR signal, without GS or glide path).

On the other hand, we find the "precision" approaches known as PA (Precision Approach). This cartographic group is based on a single approximation support system, the ILS (Instrument Landing System). The ILS system guides the aircraft in its horizontal and vertical navigation to a minimum altitude lower than NPA charts. They are divided into three categories, being: ILS CAT1, ILS CAT2 and ILS CAT3.

We can find everything related to this system in our specific manual on this topic ILS CAT I-II-III. An extensive and vital topic that requires a complete manual for detailed development. Get it at www.baeronautica.com

In short, we can find two types of approaches. Let's look at the following graph to affirm this concept and then we will study each of them:

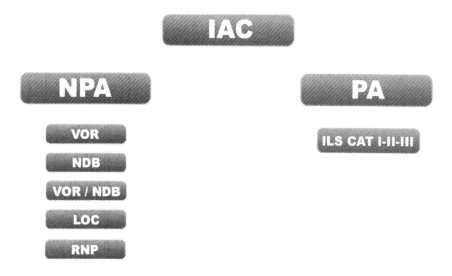

Let's start with the NPA charts. Let's analyze its symbology and operation in various situations.

Non-precision Approach Charts (NPA)

As we mentioned in previous pages, the NPA charts are based on radio navigation aids and offer guidance on the horizontal navigation of the aircraft during its approach route to a maximum point where the aircraft could descend and approach the runway without jeopardizing flight safety. For this reason, there are charts based on radio aids such as: VOR, NDB and ILS only in their navigation or horizontal flight reference. On the other hand, there is the possibility that within the same NPA approach chart several radio navigation aids will be used, for example: a VOR/NDB, VOR/LOC, NDB/LOC chart.

Each of these charts can be accompanied by an additional aid that is the measurement of the distance taken with DME equipment and associated with a radio help. Finally, there is a possibility that NPA charts will start with an instrumental procedure but end with a visual approach to the runway. That is, they start based on a reference of a certain help radius and end with a visual approximation procedure, both detailed in the chart as appropriate.

Analysis and Symbology of VOR charts (NPA)

Let's start by analysing the simplest charts and then move on to the most complex ones.

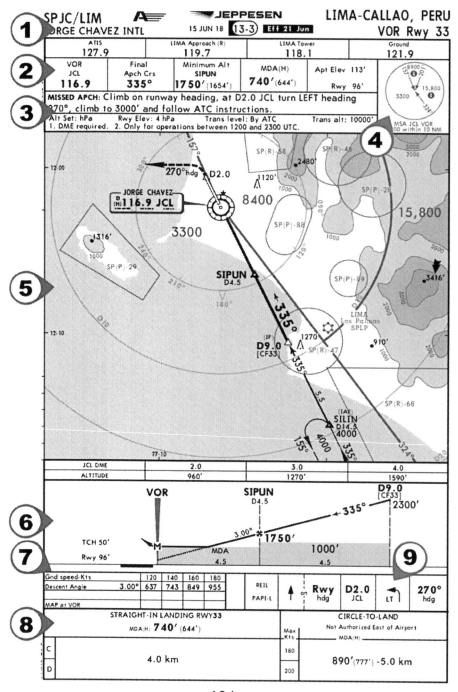

Starting from point number one, we find a traditional header with the information about the airport, the date of preparation of the chart and its respective number, information about the city and the country and, unlike the charts seen so far, here is added the information about the type of chart to be used and the runway associated with that chart. In this case, it is a VOR chart for runway 33 (VOR Rwy 33).

The second section (point two), mentions frequencies, courses and altitudes. In the first line the frequency of the ATIS, then the approach frequency, then the tower frequency and finally the frequency of the surface control. This responds to a logical order of operation, that is, they are placed in the correct order in which the pilot should use them, first he must listen to the ATIS, then communicate with the approach control so that they authorize their flight, then move to the tower frequency to authorize their landing and finally move to the frequency of the surface control to be authorized to shoot to the final position.

Just below the communication frequencies, it indicates the frequency of the radio helps to use, the final course of approach a minimum altitude at a certain point in the final section and the minimum altitude to which the aircraft can descend on this approach, known as MDA(H). This minimum altitude usually coincides with the point where the pilot must decide whether to continue with the approach with the runway in sight, or whether to make a frustrated approach as detailed in the next point. In both NPA and PAs, this final decision point is determined by a minimum altitude and a distance to the radio help. In both charts, this point is called MAP or "Missed Approach Point", with the exception that in the NPA, the MAP is given by an MDA (Minimum Descend Altitude) and in the PA it is given by a DA (Decision Altitude). The difference between these two minimum altitudes is that in the MDA only the descent must be stopped but the flight could be continued for a certain additional section, while in the DA it is necessary to make the decision to continue with the landing or make a frustrated approach.

In the third section, the frustrated approach procedure is described in clear text, detailing each step to follow for its realization. Just below this description, we find an informative box about the transition altitude and any restrictions that the chart may have, in our particular case, the chart is the mandatory requirement of a DME team with the legend "DME Required".

Finally, in the fourth section, as we have seen in the previous chart, the MSA of the sector is described with a certain reference.

In point number five, it presents the graphic view as we have seen it in the SID and STAR charts, but with the exception that a path is plotted from a starting point known as IAF (Initial Approach Fix) to an end point or MAP.

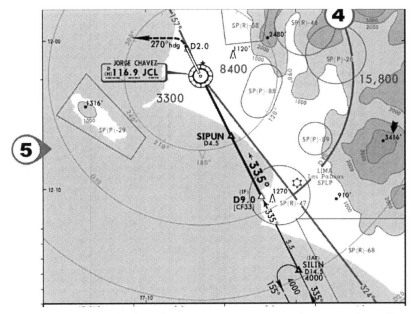

This particular chart proposes to start the procedure from the SILIN position where there is a waiting procedure and a restriction of 4000FT to D14.5 JCL.

- In addition to the information on the route or flight route, there are other additional data such as:

- Frequency of the VOR

- Elevations (the black arrow indicates the highest point and its altitude in FT)

- Additional geographical areas

- Path of the frustrated approach (dotted line)

127

In this view of horizontal navigation, there are no data or references of vertical navigation or descent profile, but there are other relevant data for the approach, such as the points by which the aircraft should fly: SILIN - D9.0 - SIPUN - JCL. Here we already have our first reference for the approach. At the next point, we will find the reference of the glide path to complete the descent. Let's see:

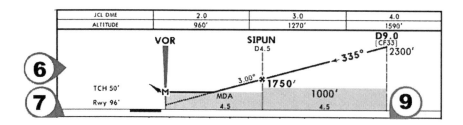

In this sixth point, a descent profile is shown that begins at D9.0 at 2300FT. From there he describes that you must continue with course 335° in descent to 1750FT to SIPUN to D4.5, then continue the descent to the MDA and reach the MAP which is identified in all charts with chart M. Just below the MAP we see a black rectangle that represents the surface of the runway and on its left two legends, one that indicates the elevation of the runway 96FT (Rwy 96') and the other indicates the height with which the threshold of the runway must be crossed, TCH (Threshold Crossing HEIGHT)

As an additional help to the graph of the descent profile proposed by the chart, in point number seven we find a reference with values set for a standard descent. Let's see:

This information is based on the speed of the approach and the vertical speed that the aircraft should take to meet the descent profile to the MAP. For example, if the aircraft has a final approach speed of 140KT, it should adopt a vertical descent speed regime of 743FT/MIN to be able to comply with the published profile.

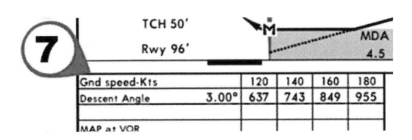

At the end of the chart, in point number eight we find the tables of operational limitations. The upper box again informs the minimum MDA(H) or "altitude" to be met while just next to it another value is presented in parentheses indicating the same information but expressed in minimum "Height" to be met. Finally, in its box below it informs the minimum visibility required to be able to legally carry out this procedure.

REMEMBER: MDA describes "Minimum Descent ALTITUDE" and MDH describes "minimum Descent HEIGHT).

Finally, we arrived at section number nine. Here the frustrated approach procedure is again described but expressed in a graph of symbols that describe the same thing that was mentioned verbatim in point 3. In this case, it indicates ascending on a runway course to D2.0 JCL, then turning from the left to 270° heading.

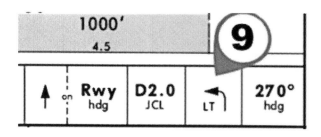

So far we have analyzed this first VOR chart, which has presented a one-step approach, that is, of a single flight that started from SILIN already facing the runway in the final approach. But it is common to find approaches of two, three steps, or more.

Most VOR procedures have 2 steps, where for each of these steps a flight path away from the airport and descent to a certain altitude and an approach path to the airport are proposed, also with a scheduled descent until reaching the final section of the bow approach to the MAP. Although these procedures involve twice as much attention as the one seen above, they do not present greater complexity of operation since it is only an approximation that requires a little more time. Let's look at an example:

130

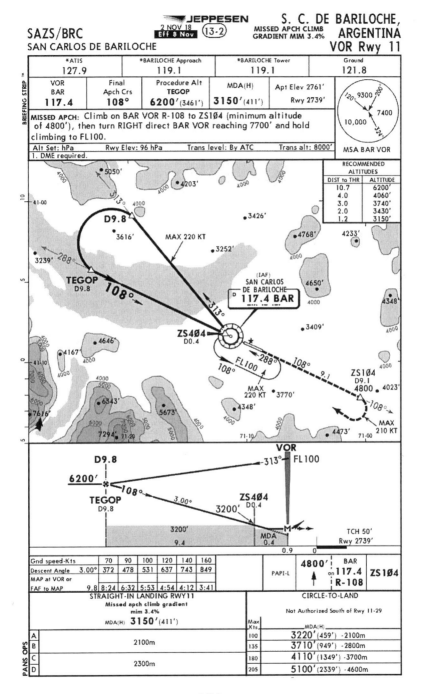

We arrived at the international airport of the City of San Carlos de Bariloche, Argentina (SAZS). Here we find a two-stage chart, as we mentioned earlier. The first informative section of the chart responds to an identical format to the previous chart from the City of Lima, PERU (SPJC).

SAZS/BRC SAN CARLOS DE BARILOCHE	JEPPESEN 2 NOV 18 Eff 8 Nov (13-2)		S. C. DE BARILOCHE, ARGENTINA VOR Rwy 11 MISSED APCH CLIMB GRADIENT MIM 3.4%
*ATIS 127.9	*BARILOCHE Approach 119.1	*BARILOCHE Tower 119.1	Ground 121.8
VOR BAR 117.4	Final Apch Crs 108°	Procedure Alt TEGOP 6200'(3461')	MDA(H) 3150'(411')	Apt Elev 2761' Rwy 2739'	120° 9300 200° 7400 10,000 320° MSA BAR VOR
MISSED APCH: Climb on BAR VOR R-108 to ZS104 (minimum altitude of 4800'), then turn RIGHT direct BAR VOR reaching 7700' and hold climbing to FL100.				
Alt Set: hPa 1. DME required.	Rwy Elev: 96 hPa	Trans level: By ATC	Trans alt: 8000'

It presents an informative heading detailing the VOR chart for runway 11 (VOR Rwy 11), a row of frequencies in a logical order of use, a row of information on radio aids, courses and minimum altitudes (including the MDA), a third informative row that describes the missed approach procedure, a fourth row related to information on transition latitude and a fifth row reporting on On the right, the MSA box of the sector. So far without any variation from the previous chart, except for their respective values.

The main difference with the previous chart is based on two special sections, the graphic view and the view of the descent profile, being the horizontal plane and vertical plane of the chart. Let's see:

Let's start by analysing the first box in the upper right margin, which refers to additional information on the recommended minimum altitudes at the aforementioned distances. Additional information typical of the areas surrounded by mountains such as this region of Argentina, surrounded by the Andes Mountain Range. The first thing we must identify when reading a chart is the location of the IAF. In this case, point number two.

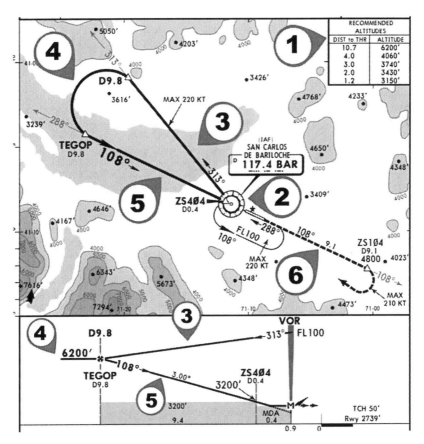

From the IAF let's continue with the numerical sequence in parallel with the two views, the horizontal plane and the vertical plane.

Point number three proposes the first section of the procedure with a distance by R313BAR up to 9.8NM and downhill to 6200FT, with a speed restriction of MAX 220KT. At point number four, the horizontal profile indicates a turn to the left and the vertical profile does not indicate descent, so it will be a shift at a level while maintaining 6200FT. Point number five leaves us at the end of runway 29 and indicates entering by R288BAR with a 108° course and from 9.8NM start the descent to the MAP looking for an MDA of 3150FT but crossing the ZS040 position at no less than 3200FT. Once you have arrived at the MAP, make the decision to continue or make a frustrated approach.

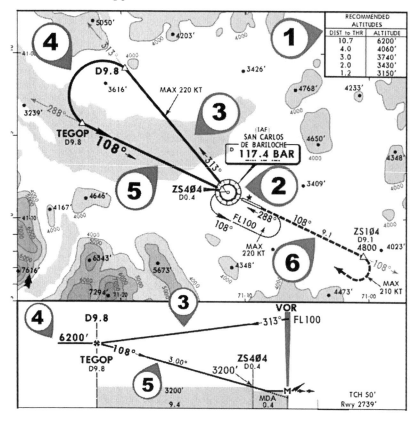

Finally, we see the lower section of the chart. In point one we find an information table on the vertical speed indicated based on the speed of approach that the aircraft plans to carry, such as the previous chart, but adding value to the estimated time that could take to fly from the FAF (final approach fi) to the MAP.

Gnd speed-Kts		70	90	100	120	140	160
Descent Angle	3.00°	372	478	531	637	743	849
MAP at VOR or FAF to MAP	9.8	8:24	6:32	5:53	4:54	4:12	3:41

	STRAIGHT-IN LANDING RWY 11
	Missed apch climb gradient mim 3.4%
	MDA(H) **3150'**(411')
A	2100m
B	
C	2300m
D	

	PAPI-L	4800' BAR on 117.4 R-108	ZS104

		CIRCLE-TO-LAND
		Not Authorized South of Rwy 11-29
Max Kts		MDA(H)
100		3220'(459') -2100m
135		3710'(949') -2800m
180		4110'(1349') -3700m
205		5100'(2339') -4600m

In point number two we find again information regarding the frustrated approach procedure. In point number three, a clarification about the MDA(H) and the minimum horizontal visibility is just below. Finally, in point number four we find information on the visual circulation for runway 11, which indicates that the procedure is not authorized south of the runway and informs the new MDA according to the speed.

Having understood the two-step VOR chart, let's look at another variant of these procedures using a radio help such as the VOR. Let's travel to the city of Rio de Janeiro and get to know one of its VOR approaches.

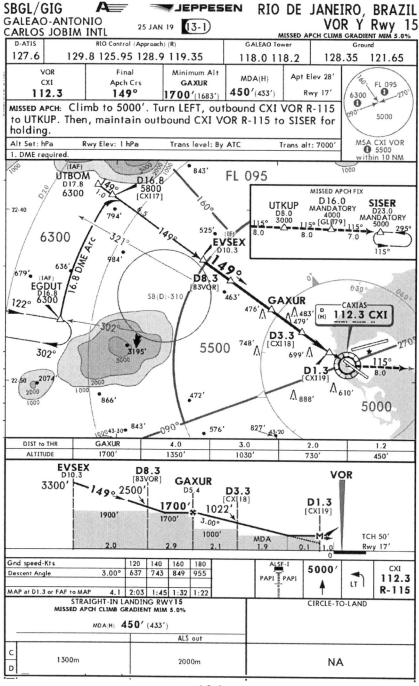

Let's start with the first section of the chart, the header and its information rows. This section is presented in the same way as the previous chart, but with an optional addition in the second row, in the second communications box. The information about Rio Control offers 4 different communication frequencies. This is due to the high demand for approaches to this airport. In the final section, the control can ask you to contact any of them and even after you change the frequency.

SBGL/GIG GALEAO-ANTONIO CARLOS JOBIM INTL	25 JAN 19 (13-1) JEPPESEN		RIO DE JANEIRO, BRAZIL VOR Y Rwy 15 MISSED APCH CLIMB GRADIENT MIN 5.0%			
D-ATIS	RIO Control (Approach) (R)		GALEAO Tower		Ground	
127.6	129.8 125.95 128.9 119.35		118.0 118.2		128.35 121.65	
VOR CXI **112.3**	Final Apch Crs **149°**	Minimum Alt GAXUR **1700'**(1683')	MDA(H) **450'**(433')	Apt Elev 28' Rwy 17'	6300 FL 095 270° 090° 5000	
MISSED APCH: Climb to 5000'. Turn LEFT, outbound CXI VOR R-115 to UTKUP. Then, maintain outbound CXI VOR R-115 to SISER for holding.						
Alt Set: hPa	Rwy Elev: 1 hPa	Trans level: By ATC		Trans alt: 7000'	MSA CXI VOR 5500 within 10 NM	
1. DME required.						

The remaining rows present traditional information about radio aids, courses, MDA, MSA, frustrated approach and finally an operational restriction, the obligation of the DME team to perform this procedure. DME required!

REMEMBER: MDA describes "Minimum Descent ALTITUDE" and MDH describes "minimum Descent HEIGHT).

Let's look at the horizontal view along with the vertical profile to analyze this procedure in the same way as the previous chart:

The first consideration of this chart is that it has two starting points, that is, two IAFs, one in the EGDUT position and the other in the UTBOM position. The procedure could begin on any of them and will depend on the location of the aircraft before the start. The second consideration is point number two, where an ARCO DME is presented to continue the procedure if it was initiated from the EGDUT position. After the ARCO, the procedure requests to enter by R329CXI with course 149° to the EVSEX position (FAF) and from there start the descent profile.

REMEMBER: the FAF or Final Approach Fix is the point where the descent begins and the final approach to the runway. This point is represented in the vertical profile or descent profile of the chart and is identified with a "malt cross" just before the final descent. Let's see:

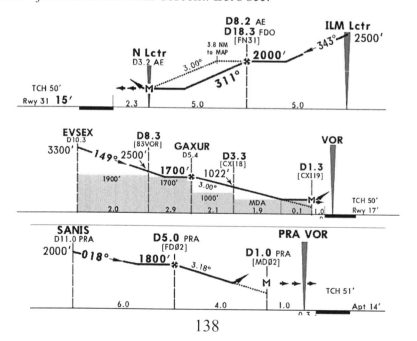

YOUR TURN! Observe the numerical sequence and continue with the procedure until you make a frustrated approach!

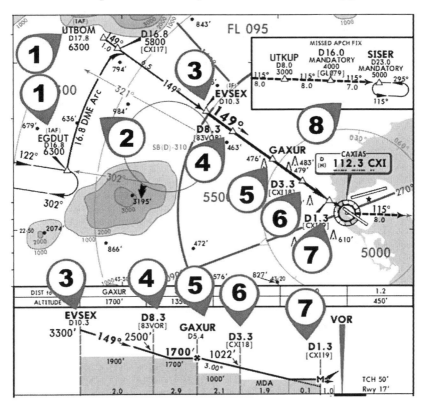

Analysis and Symbology NDB charts (NPA)

Let's change the radio help and perform a different procedure with an NDB. One of the disadvantages of these procedures is that they do not have DME equipment associated with radio help. This condition means that the chart does not offer distances to the radio help but distances by sections, or distances based on other radio aids. Let's go back to the city of Buenos Aires and see an example:

SABE/AEP — BUENOS AIRES, ARGENTINA
JORGE NEWBERY AEROPARQUE
JEPPESEN 19 OCT 18 (46-3) No. 6
FROM QUILMES **LOCATOR OR GNSS Rwy 31**

*ATIS Spanish	English	AEROPARQUE Approach	AEROPARQUE Tower	Ground
127.6	127.9	120.6	118.85	121.9

Lctr N	Final Apch Crs	Minimum Alt D8.2 AE D18.3 FDO	MDA(H)	Apt Elev 18'
375	311°	2000' (1985')	790' (775')	Rwy 31 15'

MSA N Lctr: 3000'

MISSED APCH: Climbing RIGHT turn to 3000', and follow instructions from CONTROL.

Alt Set: hPa | Rwy Elev: 1 hPa | Trans level: By ATC | Trans alt: 3000'

[Approach plan view with SAN FERNANDO 114.4 FDO, TAC 32 LOC DME 109.5 AE, AEROPARQUE 375 N, D3.2 AE, D8.2 AE, D18.3 FDO [FN31], (IAF) QUILMES 210 ILM, courses 311° and 343°]

Profile:
- TCH 50', Rwy 31 15'
- N Lctr D3.2 AE
- D8.2 AE / D18.3 FDO [FN31] 3.8 NM to MAP 2000'
- ILM Lctr 2500'
- 3.00° / 311° / 343°
- 2.3 | 5.0 | 5.0

Gnd speed-Kts	70	90	100	120	140	160
Descent angle 3.00°	372	478	531	637	743	849
MAP at N Lctr/D3.2 AE or FAF to MAP 5.0	4:17	3:20	3:00	2:30	2:09	1:53

AVASI — 3000' RT

STRAIGHT-IN LANDING RWY31
MDA(H) 790' (775')

	Max Kts		
A		A	
B		B	NA
C	4200m	C	

CIRCLE-TO-LAND

Start with a traditional header and mention the type of chart to use: LOCATOR (NDB) or GNSS (Satellite Navigation) for runway 31. Then the informative rows continue with information similar to the previous chart but add a double frequency of ATIS, one for each language.

SABE/AEP			JEPPESEN BUENOS AIRES, ARGENTINA 19 OCT 18 (46-3)			No. 6
JORGE NEWBERY AEROPARQUE				FROM QUILMES LOCATOR OR GNSS Rwy 31		
*ATIS Spanish 127.6	English 127.9	AEROPARQUE Approach 120.6		AEROPARQUE Tower 118.85		Ground 121.9
Lctr N 375		Final Apch Crs 311°	Minimum Alt D8.2 AE D18.3 FDO 2000' (1985')	MDA(H) 790' (775')	Apt Elev 18' Rwy 31 15'	3000'
MISSED APCH: Climbing RIGHT turn to 3000', and follow instructions from CONTROL.						
Alt Set: hPa		Rwy Elev: 1 hPa	Trans level: By ATC		Trans alt: 3000'	MSA N Lctr

This procedure is based on the operation with the radio beacon N located in the vicinity of SABE runway 31. To make the approach, the chart proposes to use three additional beacons, the ILS system locator, the NDB of Quilmes and the VOR of San Fernando, two locations near the city of Buenos Aires.

Any chart based on an NDB must be flown with courses with respect to the beacons, that is, with QDR and QDM. A traditional operation, something old but still effective. Note that this procedure does not declare distances between each section with respect to the NDB beacons, but it does with respect to the VOR FDO and the LOC AE. Let's look at the horizontal and vertical planes to understand this type of cartography and its variables:

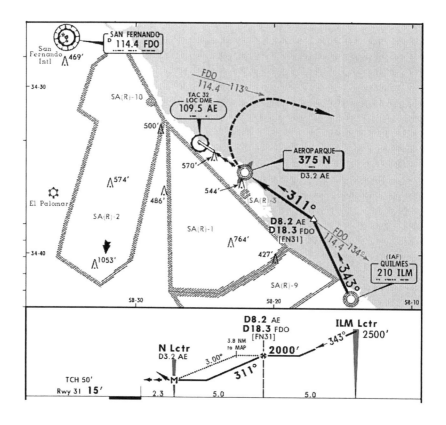

In the first instance, we need to locate the IAF that is right above the NDB ILM. From there it indicates to continue with course 343° (or QDR 343 ILM) in descent until 2000FT until you reach the FAF, located on R134FDO at D18.3NM. We can identify the FAF by its characteristic malt cross in the descent profile. After the FAF, the approach continues to enter the N beacon with course 311° (or QDM 311 ILM) and in final descent to the MDA of 790FT on the MAP located at D3.2AE. From there, two options, continue with the visual landing on runway 31 or make a frustrated approach as described in the information section.

Finally, in the lower section, we find again the information table on the vertical speed (V/S) and flight time from the FAF to the MAP. Just below, we find again the MDA(H) and the minimum horizontal visibility required for this procedure. To the right of this section, is an additional reminder of the frustrated approach procedure. Note that this procedure does NOT offer visual circulation for runway 13.

Gnd speed-Kts		70	90	100	120	140	160		AVASI	3000' RT
Descent angle	3.00°	372	478	531	637	743	849			
MAP at N Lctr/D3.2 AE or FAF to MAP	5.0	4:17	3:20	3:00	2:30	2:09	1:53			
		STRAIGHT-IN LANDING RWY31							CIRCLE-TO-LAND	
		MDA(H) **790'** (775')						Max Kts		
A								A		
B		4200m						B	NA	
C								C		

YOUR TURN AGAIN! Let's look at the following NBD approach chart from the "El Alto" airport in the city of La Paz, Bolivia (one of the highest airports in the world)!

Based on what you have learned so far, try to understand this chart and its procedure. Remember that this is a two-step chart and that we must start with the header and its rows, then move on to the analysis of the horizontal and vertical view as a whole, locating the IAF and following the route that the plane should take in its two planes (horizontal and vertical). Finally, we must analyze the lower section with the MDA(H), the visibility limitations and the options for visual circulation along with the frustrated approach procedure. Everything is ready! Let's go to La Paz airport!

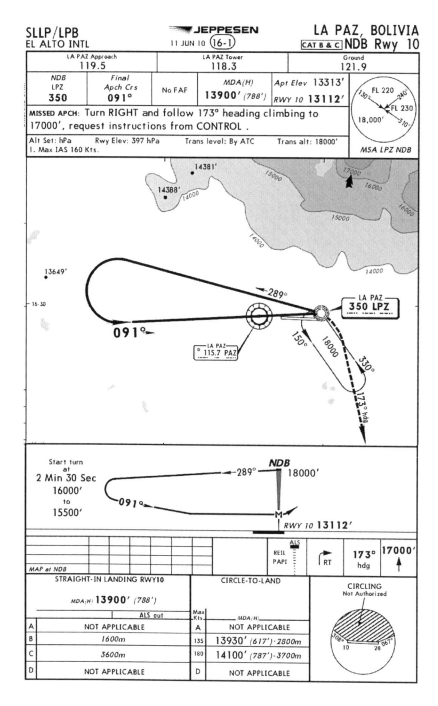

Analysis and Symbology LOC charts (NPA)

Continuing with the NPA charts, one of the most accurate options within this group is the LOC charts. This type of mapping uses the signal of the ILS system but only in its horizontal navigation, leaving aside vertical or plane descent navigation.

As we have learned in our ILS CAT I-II-III manual, the ILS system has two references, which together form an adequate flight path to guide the aircraft to the threshold of the runway, even to land without visibility. being: ILS CAT1, ILS CAT2 and ILS CAT3.

We can find everything related to this system in our specific manual on this topic ILS CAT I-II-III. An extensive and vital topic that requires a complete manual for detailed development. Get it at www.baeronautica.com

In the LOC charts, we will take only the horizontal navigation guide for the approach and the slope of descent will be expressed in distance values, as we have seen so far in the NPA. Let's travel to Madrid airport and get to know a LOC approach:

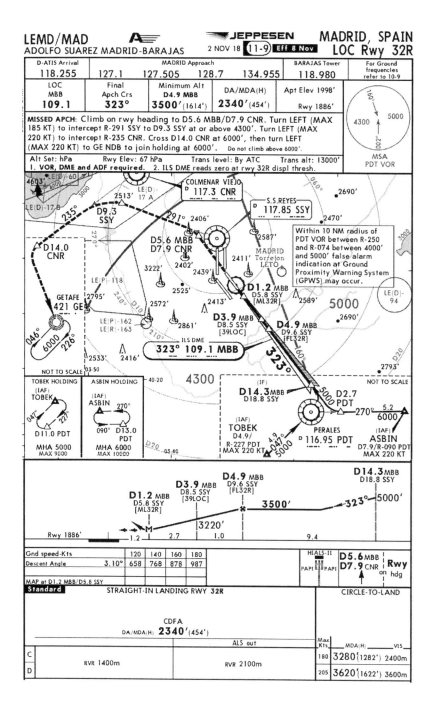

Looking at the first section, we notice a traditional heading with the clarification that this chart is a LOC Rwy32R chart. In the following rows, frequencies, altitude courses, MSA, frustrated approach and a requirement to perform this procedure. What is it?

Let's move on to the graphic plane and its vertical profile to analyze the caveats of this LOC chart:

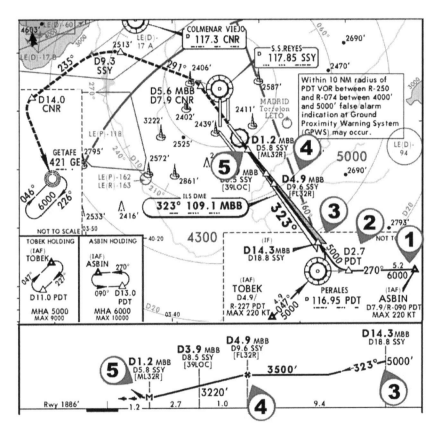

In the first instance, we must locate the IAF. Here we find two IAFs in different positions, one in TOBEK and one in ASBIN. Let's start from this last point.

From ASBIN the procedure continues like any other, with a course and a distance to the next point. Course 270°, 5.2NM at 6000FT up to D2.7PDT. From both ASBIN and TOBEK, both FAIs converge at a common point, right where the descent begins, point D14.3MBB, that is, 14.3NM of the VOR MBB. From this point, it begins the work together with the two profiles, the horizontal and the vertical, in the same way as in the previous charts, with the exception that since it is a LOC chart, the accuracy of navigation in the horizontal plane will be much greater than that which can be presented with a traditional VOR chart, since the LOC reference uses the signal of the ILS system for the horizontal flight guide.

When we arrive at the MAP, let's try to decipher the frustrated approximation procedure by interpreting the diagram presented in the vertical plane. After the VOR begins a flight route is represented by an intermittent line that flies in the same direction as the runway up to 5.6NM of MBB. From there, turn left towards 291° to 9.3NM of the VOR SSY. Posterior, shift from left to heading 233° to 14.0NM of the VOR CNR and finally, turn from left direct towards the NDB GE, where there is a waiting procedure on position 226 of this NDB. All this, in a continuous climb up to 6000FT.

Reading the description of this procedure in the upper section of the chart, we will find additional restrictions that are not graphic in the drawing but that are presented on a mandatory basis.

Finally, and unlike the rest of the charts, in the final section of this one, we find information regarding the minimums of visibility to perform the procedure but expressed in a new value such as the RVR or "Runway Visual Range". The operation will be limited to a minimum of RVR 1400Mts, or a minimum of RVR2100 Mts if the ALS (approach lighting System) is inoperative.

		ALS out	Max Kts	MDA(H)	VIS
C	RVR 1400m	RVR 2100m	180	3280 (1282')	2400m
D			205	3620 (1622')	3600m

VOR-NDB-LOC Combined Charts (NPA)

Continuing with the NPA charts, let's now look at the combined procedures where various radio aids are used during the approach until we reach the FAF. The combinations we can find are charts:

- *VOR/NDB*
- *LOC/NDB*
- *VOR/LOC*

Usually, the name of the chart responds to the logical order in which the beacons will be used. For example, in a VOR/LOC chart it is assumed that the remoteness section will be carried out with the VOR signal and in the entrance section at the end of the approach it will be done with the LOC signal. Let's look at an example of these combined charts:

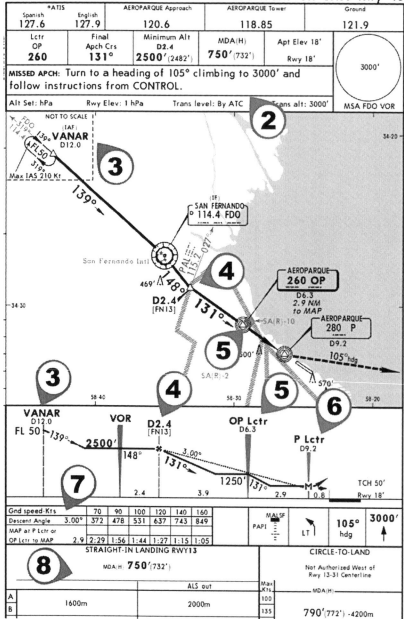

Starting with point number one, it presents a traditional header with the same information format as previous charts, but unlike them, this chart clarifies that it starts from the VANAR position and that it is a VOR DME LOCATOR (NDB) chart for runway 13. After that, the header complies with the traditional format in its next rows and without presenting operational restrictions to make this chart (point two). Let's see what happens between points three and six.

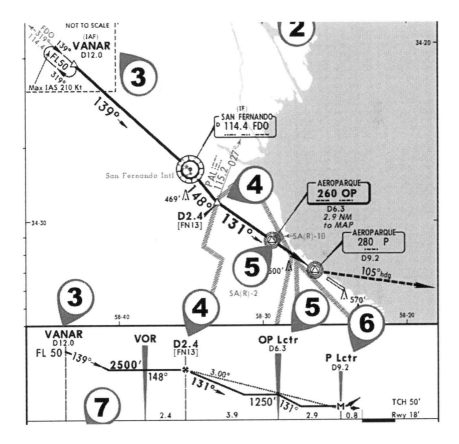

As mentioned in the header, this VOR DME LOCATOR chart initiates the procedure by flying with references to the VOR FDO from VANAR identified as the IAF and located at R319FDO

12.0NM. There is a wait for at least FL 050. Once the procedure is authorized, the aircraft begins its horizontal and vertical navigation to the next point, VOR FDO, and down to 2500FT. After the VOR FDO, continue heading 148° towards the FAF until 2.4NM of FDO. There he begins his final descent and goes on to navigate with the next beacon, the NDB OP and enters it through the QDM131 (OP entry position 311). At point number 5, the aircraft is on OP at 1250FT, just at that moment, it changes its navigation reference and begins to use the NDB P, entering it with the same course and descending to the MDA. Once you have arrived at the MAP, it is time to make the decision to continue or abandon the procedure.

Finally, in points seven and eight we find the same information that we have learned in the previous chart. An information box on vertical speed as a function of approach speed and the bottom box on visibility limitations, both in MDA and horizontal visibility. In the right margin, we find again a descriptive graph of the frustrated approximation procedure.

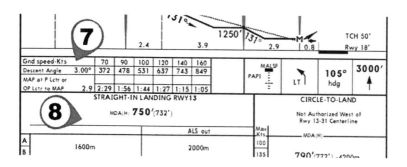

VOR-VISUAL Combined Charts (NPA)

Another strange combination of approach procedures happens when we find a chart that foresees a VOR approach but ends with a visual approach to the runway.

This scenario usually occurs when there is some geographical restriction in the area, which prevents diagramming the approach chart in such a way that it ends on a certain radial of the VOR, or when the VOR station is away from the runway to which you want to approach.

It is worth mentioning that in these special cases, the meteorological minimums are usually more restrictive to carry out the procedure since it is expected that it will end in a visual approach.

Let's travel to the city of San Martin de Los Andes, Argentina. This airport has a VOR approach and visual circulation towards the end of its runway 24 and/or 06, that is, on the same VOR approach procedure, it is expected to be completed, necessarily, visually.

Let's analyse the entirety of this chart and then describe the procedure.

SAZY — JEPPESEN SAN MARTIN DE LOS ANDES, ARGENTINA
14 DEC 18 (13-1) No.1
AVIADOR CARLOS CAMPOS   VOR DME Rwy 06/24 VISUAL CIRCLING

CHAPELCO Approach		CHAPELCO Tower	
119.6	118.2	119.6	118.2

VOR CHP	Final Apch Crs	No FAF	MDA(H) Refer to Minimums	Apt Elev 2589'	MSA CHP VOR
117.0	306°				14400 / 7500 / 8900 / 7800

MISSED APCH: Maintain 306° course to CHP VOR, then turn RIGHT to intercept CHP VOR R-360 outbound climbing to 14400' and follow instructions from control.

Alt Set: hPa   Apt Elev: 91 hPa   Trans level: By ATC   Trans alt: 8000'
1. Not authorized without DME.   2. Max IAS 180 Kts for circle to land.

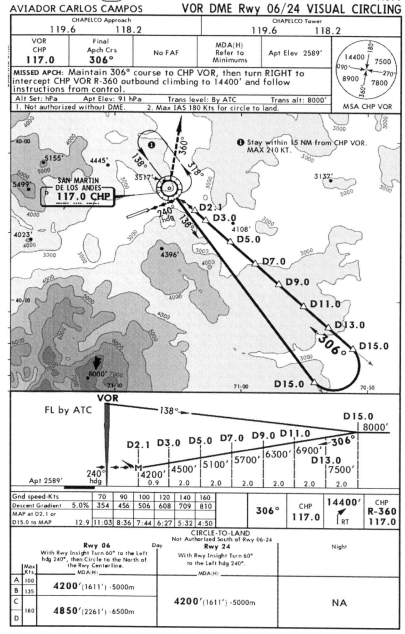

Gnd speed-Kts		70	90	100	120	140	160			
Descent Gradient	5.0%	354	456	506	608	709	810	306°	CHP 117.0	14400' RT	CHP R-360 117.0
MAP at D2.1 or D15.0 to MAP		12.9	11:03	8:36	7:44	6:27	5:32	4:50			

CIRCLE-TO-LAND
Not Authorized South of Rwy 06-24

	Max Kts	Rwy 06 Day With Rwy Insight Turn 60° to the Left hdg 240°, then Circle to the North of the Rwy Centerline. MDA(H)	Rwy 24 With Rwy Insight Turn 60° to the Left hdg 240°. MDA(H)	Night
A	100	4200'(1611') -5000m	4200'(1611') -5000m	NA
B	135			
C	180	4850'(2261') -6500m		
D				

Starting with the header we find that it presents a traditional format and information common to this section, but the description of the chart clarifies that it is a combined procedure between VOR and Visual for both runways.

SAZY	JEPPESEN	SAN MARTIN DE LOS ANDES, ARGENTINA	
	14 DEC 18 (13-1)		No.1
AVIADOR CARLOS CAMPOS		VOR DME Rwy 06/24 VISUAL CIRCLING	
CHAPELCO Approach		CHAPELCO Tower	
119.6 118.2		119.6 118.2	
VOR CHP **117.0**	Final Apch Crs **306°**	No FAF	MDA(H) Refer to Minimums	Apt Elev 2589'	14400 / 7500 090°← →270° 8900 / 7800 MSA CHP VOR
MISSED APCH: Maintain 306° course to CHP VOR, then turn RIGHT to intercept CHP VOR R-360 outbound climbing to 14400' and follow instructions from control.					
Alt Set: hPa	Apt Elev: 91 hPa	Trans level: By ATC		Trans alt: 8000'	
1. Not authorized without DME.		2. Max IAS 180 Kts for circle to land.			

The first row reports the available frequencies. The second row reports on the frequency of the VOR and the final course, clarifying that there is no FAF or MDA! The first point to keep in mind. In the absence of the MDA, he clarifies that it should refer to the minimum section. In the following rows, we find the description of the frustrated approach procedure, the MSA box of the sector and finally, the operational restrictions to carry out this procedure.

"Not Authorized without DME. Max IAS 180KT".

Let's move on to the horizontal and vertical planes. Let's analyze the step-by-step procedure and their respective considerations for this "atypical" chart.

The procedure starts from the VOR CHP. From there begins the descent to 8000FT in distance by R138CHP to D15.0 (points 1 and 2). At this point, shift from procedure from left to course 306° (R126CHP) (point3). When reaching 15.0NM again, the final descent to the MAP begins, passing through different control points and each of them with a minimum flight altitude, becoming a "staggered" descent (point 4), until reaching the MAP.

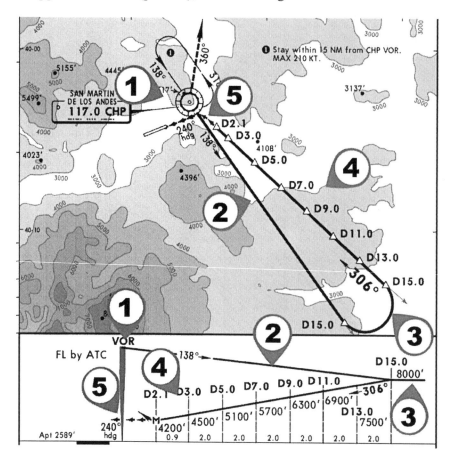

Already in the MAP, the procedure continues visually towards the runway. Let's see how follows:

Looking at the diagram more closely, we notice that right after the MAP at 2.1NM, change the drawing or symbol of the runway line for a line of arrows turning to the left directly to the runway. This line of arrows represents the path of the visual approach to runway 24 with a 240° course.

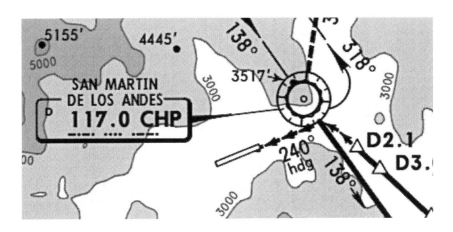

Finally, when referring to the lower section of the chart, we find the detail of the minimums and the missing MDA information in the header. YOUR TURN AGAIN!

Gnd speed-Kts		70	90	100	120	140	160	
Descent Gradient	5.0%	354	456	506	608	709	810	**306°**
MAP at D2.1 or D15.0 to MAP	12.9	11:03	8:36	7:44	6:27	5:32	4:50	

		Rwy 06	Day	CIRCLE-TO-LAND Not Authorized South of Rwy 06-24 Rwy 24
		With Rwy Insight Turn 60° to the Left hdg 240°, then Circle to the North of the Rwy Centerline.		With Rwy Insight Turn 60° to the Left hdg 240°.
	Max Kts	MDA(H)		MDA(H)
A	100	4200'(1611') -5000m		
B	135			
C	180	4850'(2261') -6500m		4200'(1611') -5000m
D				

ILS Approach Chart (PA)

As we mentioned at the beginning of this chapter, ILS procedures are extreme precision procedures that guide the aircraft, horizontally and vertically, to the threshold of the runway, and even in some cases, allow it to make an automatic landing without visibility.

These ILS procedures are divided into three categories of operation according to the established minimums, these are:

- ILS Category I
- ILS Category II
- ILS Category III

We can find everything related to this system in our specific manual on this topic ILS CAT I-II-III. An extensive and vital topic that requires a complete manual for detailed development. Get it at www.baeronautica.com

Like the previous chart, ILS procedures can have one, two, three steps or more, as required by the geography of the terrain and the arrangement of the airport. We will start by analyzing a simple ILS chart and then we will add more complexity as we move forward. Let's see:

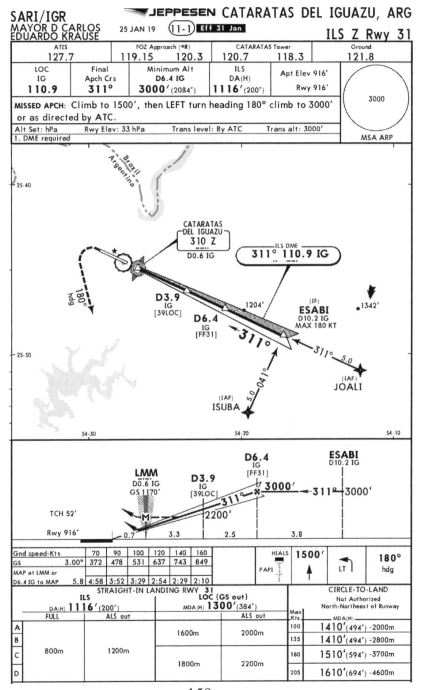

Welcome to the city of Iguazú, Argentina. Cradle of one of the "Wonders of the World", the famous "Iguazu Falls". Let's start by analyzing the header. The format is similar to the previous ones seen but with some caveats to consider.

SARI/IGR MAYOR D CARLOS EDUARDO KRAUSE		JEPPESEN CATARATAS DEL IGUAZU, ARG			
	25 JAN 19 (11-1) Eff 31 Jan			❶ ILS Z Rwy 31	
ATIS 127.7	FOZ Approach (*R) 119.15 120.3	CATARATAS Tower 120.7	118.3		Ground 121.8
LOC IG 110.9	Final Apch Crs 311°	Minimum Alt D6.4 IG 3000' (2084')	ILS DA(H) 1116' (200') ❷	Apt Elev 916' Rwy 916'	3000
MISSED APCH: Climb to 1500', then LEFT turn heading 80° climb to 3000' or as directed by ATC.					
Alt Set: hPa	Rwy Elev: 33 hPa	Trans level: By ATC		Trans alt: 3000'	MSA ARP
1. DME required					

In the description of the procedure, point number one, it is already described that it is an ILS procedure for runway 31 and gives it the name Zulu. Another major difference from the previous charts is point 2, where a minimum altitude called DA(H) is reported. In the previous chart, the MDA referred to the minimum altitude of descent, here, the DA fulfills a similar function but refers to an altitude (or height) of decision, hence its name DA(H) "Decision Altitude (Height)". The main difference between an MDA and a DA is that in the first one there is no obligation to make the decision, you just have to stop the descent to the minimum distance to the runway and then decide. On the other hand, in the DA "THE DECISION MUST BE MADE" to continue or abort the approach.

The rest of the heading presents traditional information, as we have already learned in the previous chart. In this particular case, there is an operational restriction. YOUR TURN to find out what it is! Now let's move on to the view of the horizontal and vertical planes:

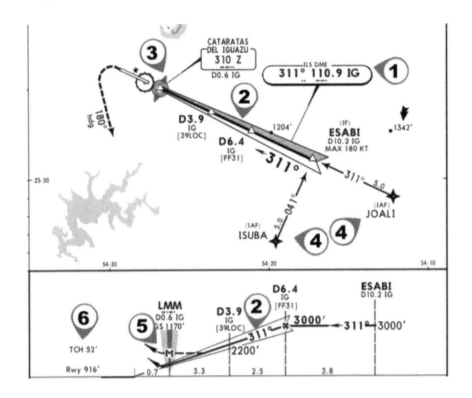

Point 1 represents the main beacon of the chart, which, unlike the others, is framed and with a black shading, which represents its "Main" character. Point 2 represents the ILS trajectory with a triangle in the vertical and horizontal plane, unlike NPAs that only represented the trajectory with a straight line. Point 3 is considered a support beacon and/or aid to the main one. At point 4, we find two FAIs and both converge in the ESABI position. Point 5 represents the MAP just above the Z beacon. Finally, point six represents the crossing height of the threshold. YOUR TURN!

At the end of the chart, we find information similar to the previous chart. In point 1, an information box on the vertical speed is a function of the approach speed. The frustrated approach procedure is shown in point 2. Point 3 describes the new altitudes for visual circulation. Section 4 details the minimum visibility to perform this procedure. And at point 5, we will stop for a moment to analyse your information.

Gnd speed-Kts		70	90	100	120	140	160		HIALS	1500'		180°
GS	3.00°	372	478	531	637	743	849	①	PAPI		LT	hdg
MAP at LMM or D6.4 IG to MAP	5.8	4:58	3:52	3:29	2:54	2:29	2:10					
		STRAIGHT-IN LANDING RWY 31								CIRCLE-TO-LAND		
		ILS				LOC (GS out)				Not Authorized North-Northeast of Runway		
	DA(H)	1116'(200')			MDA(H)	1300'(384')		②	Max Kts	MDA(H)		
	FULL		ALS out	⑤		ALS out			100	1410'(494') -2000		③
A					1600m		2000m		135	1410'(494') -2800m		
B												
C	800m		1200m						180	1510'(594') -3700m		
D				④	1800m		2200m		205	1610'(694') -4600m		

Here we notice that two minimum altitudes are reported, a DA typical of a PA or ILS chart, but an MDA, typical of an NPA chart, is also reported. In this case, the DA will be used when the ILS system works in its entirety, providing guidance on the horizontal profile (LOC) and the vertical profile (GS), becoming a precision chart. If the GS is inoperative, the chart could only consider the use of the LOC, that is, it would only assist as a guide to horizontal navigation, so it would not be a precision chart, since it has been transformed into an NPA LOC. It is because of this transformation that your DA has also become and is now an MDA.

Let's look at another example to better assimilate these learned concepts. This time let's analyse a two-step ILS:

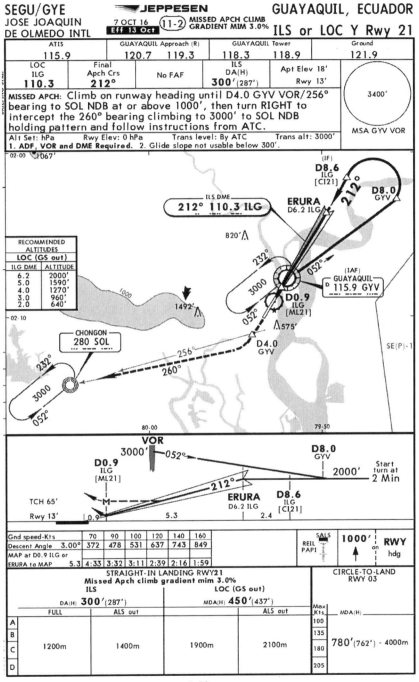

This procedure presents a traditional header with information about the airport, the date of creation of the charter, the name of the city and a description of the type of charter to be made on a certain runway.

SEGU/GYE		JEPPESEN		GUAYAQUIL, ECUADOR	
JOSE JOAQUIN DE OLMEDO INTL	7 OCT 16 Eff 13 Oct	(11-2) MISSED APCH CLIMB GRADIENT MIM 3.0%		ILS or LOC Y Rwy 21	
ATIS 115.9	GUAYAQUIL Approach (R) 120.7 119.3		GUAYAQUIL Tower 118.3 118.9		Ground 121.9
LOC ILG 110.3	Final Apch Crs 212°	No FAF	ILS DA(H) 300'(287')	Apt Elev 18' Rwy 13'	3400' MSA GYV VOR
MISSED APCH: Climb on runway heading until D4.0 GYV VOR/256° bearing to SOL NDB at or above 1000', then turn RIGHT to intercept the 260° bearing climbing to 3000' to SOL NDB holding pattern and follow instructions from ATC.					
Alt Set: hPa Rwy Elev: 0 hPa Trans level: By ATC Trans alt: 3000' 1. ADF, VOR and DME Required. 2. Glide slope not usable below 300'.					

The first consideration of this chart is the operating restriction requested by ADF, VOR and DME in operation. On the other hand, it also clarifies that the GS signal is not usable below 300FT in height.

Moving on to the horizontal plane we find a box in the left margin, just in the middle of the diagram. This is information about the recommended altitudes when the GS signal is out of service. This information is based on reading the DME distance from the ILS system. For example, if the distance

RECOMMENDED ALTITUDES	
LOC (GS out)	
ILG DME	ALTITUDE
6.2	2000'
5.0	1590'
4.0	1270'
3.0	960'
2.0	640'

indicator shows a value of 5.0NM, the recommended altitude is 1590FT. However, if the distance is 3.5NM, values would have to be interpolated and the recommended altitude would be 1115FT. Now let's see how the horizontal plane and the vertical plane work together.

In In the first instance, we place the IAF just above GYV VOR (point one). From there, start the procedure with a distance by R052GYV to D8.0 and decreasing to 2000FT (point two). Next, turn left to the final course 212° to enter through the ILS signal to ERURA at D6.5ILG (point three). From this point, the flight begins with instrumental references of horizontal and vertical navigation, flying LOC and GS to point number 4, ILG's MAP to D0.9NM. There is the DA. Let's imagine that we decided to make a frustrated approach. To do this, the chart indicates to follow the runway course to D4.0, after direct to SOL climb to 3000FT and to perform a waiting circuit on the NDB SOL

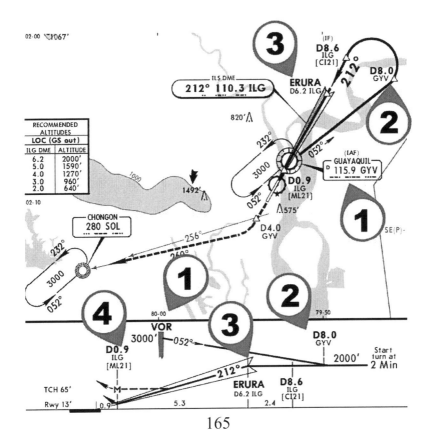

Now let's look at the final section of this ILS chart. Again, we find information about the appropriate vertical speed to meet the descent profile of the ILS. Followed by graphic information about the frustrated approach procedure. Below, the horizontal visibility limitations and the two minimum altitudes, the DA and the MDA, appear again. As we saw earlier, the DA corresponds to the use of the chart with the complete ILS system and the MDA corresponds to the use of the chart with the inoperative GS system.

Gnd speed-Kts	70	90	100	120	140	160		SALS REIL PAPI	1000' on hdg	RWY
Descent Angle 3.00°	372	478	531	637	743	849				
MAP at D0.9 ILG or										
ERURA to MAP 5.3	4:33	3:32	3:11	2:39	2:16	1:59				
	STRAIGHT-IN LANDING RWY21 Missed Apch climb gradient mim 3.0%							CIRCLE-TO-LAND RWY 03		
	ILS DA(H) 300'(287')			LOC (GS out) MDA(H) 450'(437')						
	FULL	ALS out			ALS out		Max Kts	MDA(H)		
A							100			
B							135			
C	1200m	1400m		1900m	2100m		180	780'(762') - 4000m		
D							205			

Now let's look at a more complex chart located in an area surrounded by mountains such as the City of Quito, Ecuador. A procedure full of important considerations to take into account due to the risk of operation on an IFR flight over an area surrounded by obstacles.

In principle, let's look at the complete chart and then analyze its different sections and its complete operation from the IAF. Let's see:

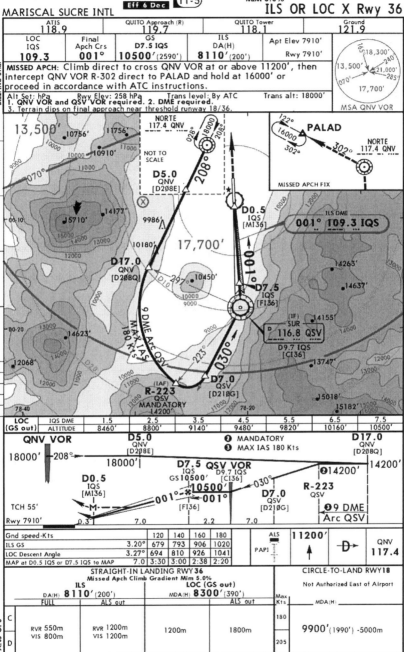

Its header has a traditional format with information about the airport, the charter, the city and the runway to be used. In addition, a clarification is added about a requirement right next to the name of the city. Its atypical location is due to the importance of this restriction and the fact that it is information that SHOULD NOT BE OMITTED!

SEQM/UIO		JEPPESEN 30 NOV 18 Eff 6 Dec (11-5)	MISSED APCH CLIMB GRADIENT MIM 5.0%	QUITO, ECUADOR	
MARISCAL SUCRE INTL				ILS OR LOC X Rwy 36	
ATIS 118.9		QUITO Approach (R) 119.7		QUITO Tower 118.1	Ground 121.9
LOC IQS 109.3	Final Apch Crs 001°	GS D7.5 IQS 10500' (2590')	ILS DA(H) 8110' (200')	Apt Elev 7910' Rwy 7910'	18,300' 13,500' 21,000' 285' 17,700'
MISSED APCH: Climb direct to cross QNV VOR at or above 11200', then intercept QNV VOR R-302 direct to PALAD and hold at 16000' or proceed in accordance with ATC instructions.					
Alt Set: hPa Rwy Elev: 258 hPa Trans level: By ATC Trans alt: 18000' 1. QNV VOR and QSV VOR required. 2. DME required. 3. Terrain dips on final approach near threshold runway 18/36.					MSA QNV VOR

Below, the header follows the informative rows without any additional consideration, showing the typical information of these rows. In the MSA box, we notice the high altitudes to take into account to fly over this area. In the last row, we find an operational restriction to make this chart, which requests that the VOR stations of QNV and QSV be in service and that the aircraft have DME equipment.

Now let's move on to the operational view with the horizontal and vertical profile of the flight. The first consideration to keep in mind is that this chart is based on 3 beacons, the QNV and QSV VOR stations and the ILS IQS system. Following this, we must consider that it is a procedure with several steps, including a decreasing DME ARC. Let's see:

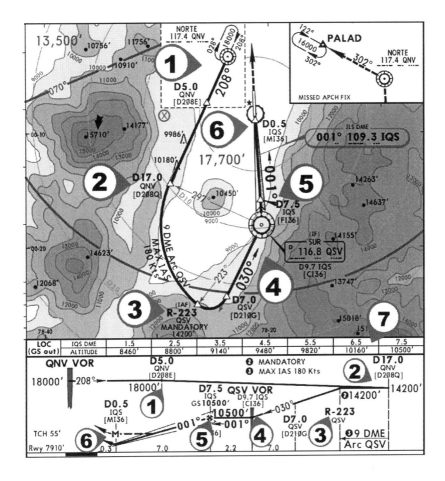

The procedure starts from the VOR QNV where we find a waiting procedure at 18000FT (point 1). From there, the flight continues 5.0NM with a course of 208°. When reaching 5.0NM, the descent begins to 14200FT, the same course until 17.0NM where the ARCO DME will begin, which has a speed restriction of MAX 180KT (point 2). Then the ARCO arrives at R223QSV, a position where the ARCO ends while maintaining 14200FT. Back, shift on the left towards the VOR QSV in descent to 10500FT (points 3 and 4).

From here, continue with course 001° towards the FAF and maintaining 1050FT (point 5). Once the FAF arrives, it begins the final approximation by references of the complete ILS, (LOC + GS), in descent to the MAP located at D0.5IQS with a DA of 8110FT or DH of 200FT (point 6).

Let's finish the Quito chart with the lower section. From left to right we find the reference box on vertical speed, followed by the representation of the light system of runway 36 and the graphic description of the frustrated approach procedure.

Gnd speed-Kts		120	140	160	180	ALS	11200'		QNV
ILS GS	3.20°	679	793	906	1020	PAPI		-D→	117.4
LOC Descent Angle	3.27°	694	810	926	1041				
MAP at D0.5 IQS or D7.5 IQS to MAP	7.0	3:30	3:00	2:38	2:20				

STRAIGHT-IN LANDING RWY 36 Missed Apch Climb Gradient Mim 5.0%				CIRCLE-TO-LAND RWY 18		
ILS DA(H) **8110'**(200') FULL	ALS out	LOC (GS out) MDA(H) **8300'**(390')	ALS out	Not Authorized East of Airport Max Kts	MDA(H)	
C	RVR 550m VIS 800m	RVR 1200m VIS 1200m	1200m	1800m	180	9900'(1990') -5000m
D					205	

In the second row, we arrive at the description of the DA(H) for the operation with the complete ILS system and for the operation only with LOC references (without GS). Finally, the minimum visibility expressed as an RVR value in meters.

Having understood the fundamental concepts of Operation ILS, let's return to the City of Lima, Peru. Here we will find a very particular ILS approach. Let's see:

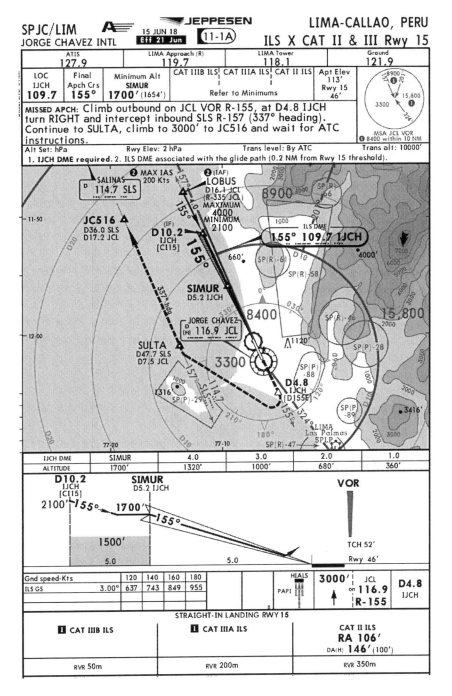

We observed a chart with several special considerations unlike the previous ones studied. Analysing the header we find the first caveats. The description of the chart indicates that it is an ILS CATEGORY II-III procedure.

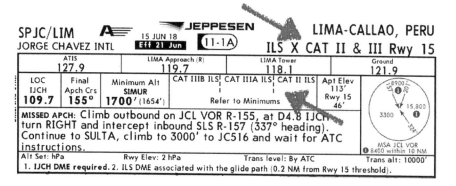

Besides, in the DA information section, we note that it is not declared as in the previous chart since ILS CAT II operations have a lower DA than the previous charts and ILS CAT III operations may not have a DA, taking the aircraft to the surface of the runway. Let's look at the final section of the chart. Here we note that in the DA section, only one value is reported for the case of ILS CAT II operations, omitting this value for ILS CAT III operations.

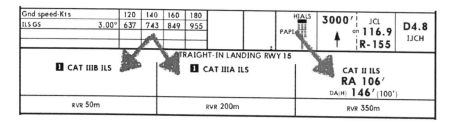

Let's see how this procedure is described to perform a CAT II or CAT III ILS. Let's pass the diagram:

This procedure turns out to be a one-step ILS, that is, it does not have a remoteness path as we have seen before. We located the IAF at the LOBUS point. From there, continue in course 155° and down to 2100FT to D10.2IJCH (distance to the ILS). At this point, we continue in the same course and in descent until 1700 in the SIMUR position. It is in this position that the complete signal of the ILS (LOC + GS) will be intercepted. From here, the flight with ILS references to the 146FT DA will be followed if it is an ILS CAT II, or until you touch the runway WITHOUT DA if it is an ILS CAT III.

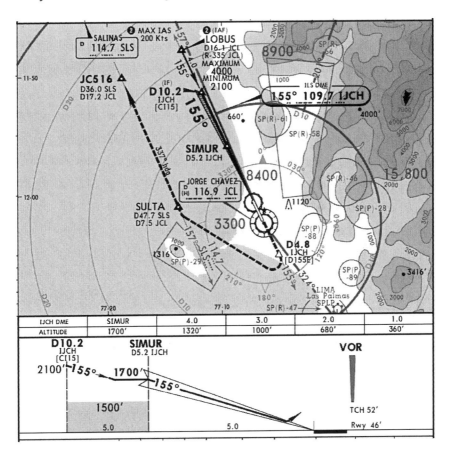

In the absence of a MAP declared in the charter, the frustrated approach procedure could be initiated at any time that the crew deems it necessary, the limit for this being the DA in the case of operation ILS CAT II and without limit in the case of operation ILS CAT III.

We can find everything related to this system in our specific manual on this topic ILS CAT I-II-III. An extensive and vital topic that requires a complete manual for detailed development. Get it at www.baeronautica.com

After understanding the benefits of an ILS CAT II and CAT III approach, we will continue in the city of Lima to learn about another of the qualities of this airport and its cartography.

Imagine that pilots experience their first approach to the airport of a certain city where the geography of the terrain may present them with certain obstacle restrictions, in this situation it would be extremely useful to know the area, or at least, the sector where it is planned to fly, such as the final approach to the runway you want to land. Considering this premise, a series of airport familiarization charts have been created, some about the airport in general and the area, as we have seen before and others specific about the final section of the runway to be used. Let's look at the menu on runway 15 in Lima:

SPJC/LIM ① **AIRPORT FAMILIARIZATION**
JORGE CHAVEZ INTL 20 MAY 16 (19-03) **LIMA-CALLAO, PERU**
Rwy 15

1. CAUTION: Birds in Vicinity of Airport
2. Mountainous Terrain East of Airport
3. Restricted and Prohibited Areas All Quadrants

| Apt Elev 113' |
| 5 NM Northwest Lima |
| S12 01.3 W077 06.9 |

MSA LIM VOR

RUNWAY 15

Caution: The runway is not grooved or crowned and is slippery when wet. Takeoff and landing performance maybe affected during or immediately after heavy rains.

Visual vertical guidance is provided by PAPI (3.0°) on the left side of the runway.

There are several obstacles, including a broadcast tower rising to 450 feet MSL, 2 NM from the departure end of this runway.

There may be simultaneous departures being conducted in the opposite direction.

This is the preferred runway for arrivals.

In the first point, we find a traditional header with information about the airport, the chart and the runway to be analyzed. In the next row, there are three boxes, one with warnings in clear text, in this case warning about the presence of birds in the vicinity, mountainous area east of the airport and restricted areas on the four quadrants. The following box provides information on the elevation and location of the airport concerning the city. And finally, the MSA box of the sector.

Secondly, a panoramic photograph of the final section of the approach to runway 15 of the airport is presented, which allows you to visualize the entire runway, the obstacles, its location concerning the city and everything visually relevant to the approach this runway for the first time.

Finally, in point three we find additional information about the runway, the PAPI system, obstacles, traffic and suggestions.

Abbreviations

A/A	Air to Air		AH	Alert Height
AAF	Army Air Field		AHP	Army Heliport
AAIM	Aircraft Autonomous Integrity Monitoring		AIRAC	Aeronautical Information Regulation and Control
AAIS	Automated Aerodrome Information Service		AIREP	Air-Report
			AIS	Aeronautical Information Services
AAL	Above Aerodrome Level		ALA	Aircraft Landing Area
AAS	Airport Advisory Service		ALF	Auxiliary Landing Field
AAU	Authorized Approach UNICOM		ALS	Approach Light System
AB	Air Base		ALS	Low Intensity Approach Lights
ABM	Abeam		ALT	Altitude
ABN	Aerodrome Beacon		ALTN	Alternate
AC	Air Carrier		AMA	Area Minimum Altitude
ACA	Arctic Control Area		AMSL	Above Mean Sea Level
ACA	Approach Control Area		ANGB	Air National Guard Base
ACAS	Airborne Collision Avoidance System		AOC	Aircraft Operator Certificate
			AOE	Airport/Aerodrome of Entry
ACARS	Airborne Communications Addressing and Reporting System		AOM	Airport Operating Minimums
			AOR	Area of Responsibility
			APAPI	Abbreviated Precision Approach Path Indicator
ACC	Area Control Center			
ACFT	Aircraft		APC	Area Positive Control
ACN	Aircraft Classification Number		APCH	Approach
AD	Aerodrome		APP	Approach Control
ADA	Advisory Area		APT	Airport
ADF	Automatic Direction Finding		APV	Approach Procedure with Vertical Guidance
ADIZ	Air Defense Identification Zone			
ADNL	Additional		AR	Authorization Required
ADR	Advisory Route		ARB	Air Reserve Base
ADS	Automatic Dependent Surveillance		ARINC	Aeronautical Radio, Inc.
ADS-B	Automatic Dependent Surveillance-Broadcast		ARO	Aerodrome Reporting Officer
			ARP	Airport Reference Point
			ARR	Arrival
ADV	Advisory Area		ARTCC	Air Route Traffic Control Center
AEIS	Aeronautical Enroute Information Service		ASDA	Accelerate Stop Distance Available
			ASMGCS	Advanced Surface Movement Guidance and Control System
AER	Approach End of Runway			
AERADIO	Air Radio		ASOS	Automated Surface Observing System
AERO	Aerodrome			
AF Aux	Air Force Auxiliary Field		ASR	Airport Surveillance Radar
AFB	Air Force Base		ATA	Actual Time of Arrival
AFIS	Aerodrome Flight Information Service		ATCAA	Air Traffic Control Assigned Airspace
AFIS	Automatic Flight Information Services (FAA)		ATCC	Air Traffic Control Center
			ATCT	Air Traffic Control Tower
AFLD	Airfield		ATD	Actual Time of Departure
AFN	American Forces Network		ATF	Aerodrome Traffic Frequency
AFRS	Armed Forces Radio Stations		ATFM	Air Traffic Flow Management
AFRU	Aerodrome Frequency Response Unit		ATIS	Automatic Terminal Information Service
AFS	Air Force Station		ATND SKD	Attended Scheduled Hours
AFSS	Automated Flight Service Station		ATS	Air Traffic Service
A/G	Air-to-Ground		ATZ	Aerodrome Traffic Zone
AGL	Above Ground Level		AU	Approach UNICOM
AGNIS	Azimuth Guidance Nose-in-Stand			

AUP	Airspace Utilization Plane	CMNPS	Canadian Minimum Navigation Performance Specification
AUTH	Authorized		
AUW	All-Up Weight	CMV	Converted Met Visibility
AUX	Auxiliary	CNF	Computer Navigation Fix
AVBL	Available	CO	County
AWIB	Aerodrome Weather Information Broadcast	COMLO	Compass Locator
		COMMS	Communications
AWIS	Aerodrome Weather Information Service	CONT	Continuous
		CONTD	Continued
AWOS	Automated Weather Observing System	COORDS	Coordinates
		COP	Change Over Point
AWSS	Aviation Weather Sensor System	CORR	Corridor
AWY	Airway	CP	Command Post
AZM	Azimuth	CPDLC	Controller Pilot Data Link Communications
Baro VNAV	Barometric Vertical Navigation		
BC	Back Course	Cpt	Clearance (Pre-Taxi Procedure)
BCM	Back Course Marker	CRC	Cyclical Redundancy Check
BCN	Beacon	CRP	Compulsory Reporting Point
BCOB	Broken Clouds or Better	CRS	Course
BCST	Broadcast	CST	Central Standard Time
BDRY	Boundary	CTA	Control Area
BLDG	Building	CTAF	Common Traffic Advisory Frequency
BM	Back Marker		
BRG	Bearing	CTL	Control
B-RNAV	Basic RNAV	CTOT	Calculated Take-off Time
BS	Broadcast Station (Commercial)	CTR	Control Zone
C	ATC IFR Flight Plan Clearance Delivery Frequency	CVFP	Charted Visual Flight Procedure
		CVFR	Controlled VFR
CADIZ	Canadian Air Defense Identification Zone	D	Day
		DA	Decision Altitude
CAE	Control Area Extension	DA (H)	Decision Altitude (Height)
CA/GRS	Certified Air/Ground Radio Service	D-ATIS	Digital ATIS
CANPA	Constant Angle Non-Precision Approach	DCL	Data Link Departure Clearance Service
CARS	Community Aerodrome Radio Station	DCT	Direct
		DECMSND	Decommissioned
CAT	Category	DEG	Degree
CBA	Cross Border Area	DEP	Departure Control/Departure Procedures
CCN	Chart Change Notices		
CDFA	Continuous Descent Final Approach	DER	Departure End of Runway
		DEWIZ	Distance Early Warning Identification Zone
CDI	Course Deviation Indicator		
CDR	Conditional Route	DF	Direction Finder
CDT	Central Daylight Time	DISPL THRESH	Displaced Threshold
CEIL	Ceiling		
CERAP	Combined Center/Radar Approach Control	DIST	Distance
		DME	Distance-Measuring Equipment
CFIT	Controlled Flight Into Terrain	DOD	Department of Defense
CGAS	Coast Guard Air Station	DOM	Domestic
CGL	Circling Guidance Lights	DP	Obstacle Departure Procedure
CH	Channel	DRCO	Dial-up Remote Communications Outlet
CH	Critical Height		
CHGD	Changed	E	East or Eastern
CL	Centerline Lights		

EAT	Expected Approach Time	FRA	Free Route Airspace
ECOMS	Jeppesen Explanation of Common Minimum Specifications	FREQ	Frequency
		FSS	Flight Service Station
EDT	Eastern Daylight Time	FT	Feet
EET	Estimated Elapsed Time	FTS	Flexible Track System
EFAS	Enroute Flight Advisory Service	G	Guards only (radio frequencies)
EFF	Effective	GA	General Aviation
EFVS	Enhanced Flight Vision System	GBAS	Ground-Based Augmentation System
EGNOS	European Geostationary Navigation Overlay Services	GCA	Ground Controlled Approach (radar)
EH	Eastern Hemisphere	GCO	Ground Communication Outlet
ELEV	Elevation	GEN	General
EMAS	Engineered Materials Arresting System	GLONASS	Global Orbiting Navigation Satellite System
EMERG	Emergency	GLS	Ground Based Augmentation System [GBAS] Landing System
ENG	Engine		
EOBT	Estimated Off Block Time	GMT	Greenwich Mean Time
EST	Eastern Standard Time	GND	Ground Control
EST	Estimated	GND	Surface of the Earth (either land or water)
ETA	Estimated Time of Arrival		
ETD	Estimated Time of Departure	GNSS	Global Navigation Satellite System
ETE	Estimated Time Enroute	GP	Glidepath
ETOPS	Extended Range Operation with two-engine airplanes	GPA	Glidepath Angle
		GPS	Global Positioning System
EVS	Enhanced Vision System	GPWS	Ground Proximity Warning System
FAA	Federal Aviation Administration	GS	Glide Slope
FACF	Final Approach Course Fix	G/S	Ground Speed
FAF	Final Approach Fix	GWT	Gross Weight
FAIL	Failure	H	Non-Directional Radio Beacon or High Altitude
FANS	Future Air Navigation System		
FAP	Final Approach Point	H24	24 Hour Service
FAR	Federal Aviation Regulation	HAA	Height Above Airport
FAS DB	Final Approach Segment Datablock	HALS	High Approach Landing System
FAT	Final Approach Track	HAS	Height Above Site
FATO	Final Approach and Take-off Area	HAT	Height Above Touchdown
FBO	Fixed Based Operator	HC	Critical Height
FCP	Final Control Point	HDG	Heading
FIA	Flight Information Area	HF	High Frequency (3-30 MHz)
FIC	Flight Information Center	HGS	Head-up Guidance System
FIR	Flight Information Region	HI	High (altitude)
FIS	Flight Information Service	HI	High Intensity (lights)
FL	Flight Level (Altitude)	HIALS	High Intensity Approach Light System
FLARES	Flare Pots or Goosenecks		
FLD	Field	HIRL	High Intensity Runway Edge Lights
FLG	Flashing	HIRO	High Intensity Runway Operations
FLT	Flight	HIWAS	Hazardous Inflight Weather Advisory Service
FM	Fan Marker		
FMC	Flight Management Computer	HJ	Sunrise to Sunset
FMS	Flight Management System	HN	Sunset to Sunrise
FOD	Foreign Object Damage	HO	By Operational Requirements
FOM	Flight Operation Manual	hPa	Hectopascal (one hectopascal = one millibar)
FPM	Feet Per Minute		
FPR	Flight Planning Requirements	HR	Hours (period of time)

HS	During Hours of Scheduled Operations
HST	High Speed Taxiway Turn-off
HSTIL	High Speed Taxiway Turn-off Indicator Lights
HUD	Head-Up Display
HUDLS	Head-Up Display Landing System
HX	No Specific Working Hours
Hz	Hertz (cycles per second)
I	Island
IAC	Instrument Approach Chart
IAF	Initial Approach Fix
IAML	Integrity Monitor Alarm
IAP	Instrument Approach Procedure
IAS	Indicated Airspeed
IATA	International Air Transport Association
IAWP	Initial Approach Waypoint
IBN	Identification Beacon
ICAO	International Civil Aviation Organization
IDENT	Identification
IF	Intermediate Fix
IFBP	Inflight Broadcast Procedure
IFR	Instrument Flight Rules
IGS	Instrument Guidance System
ILS	Instrument Landing System
IM	Inner Marker
IMAL	Integrity Monitor Alarm
IMC	Instrument Meteorological Conditions
IMTA	Intensive Military Training Area
INDEFLY	Indefinitely
IN or INS	Inches
INFO	Information
INOP	Inoperative
INS	Inertial Navigation System
INT	Intersection
INTL	International
IORRA	Indian Ocean Random RNAV Area
IR	Instrument Restricted Controlled Airspace
IS	Islands
ITWS	Integrated Terminal Weather System
I/V	Instrument/Visual Controlled Airspace
JAA	Joint Aviation Authorities
JAR-OPS	Joint Aviation Requirements–Operations
KGS	Kilograms
kHz	Kilohertz
KIAS	Knots Indicated Airspeed
KM	Kilometers
Kmh	Kilometer(s) per Hour
KT	Knots
KTAS	Knots True Airspeed
L	Locator (Compass)
LAA	Local Airport Advisory
LAAS	Local Area Augmentation System
LACFT	Large Aircraft
LAHSO	Land and Hold Short Operations
LAT	Latitude
LBCM	Locator Back Course Marker
LBM	Locator Back Marker
LBS	Pounds (Weight)
LCG	Load Classification Group
LCN	Load Classification Number
Lctr	Locator (Compass)
LDA	Landing Distance Available
LDA	Localizer-type Directional Aid
LDI	Landing Direction Indicator
LDIN	Lead-in Light System
LGTH	Length
LIM	Locator Inner Marker
LIRL	Low Intensity Runway Lights
LLWAS	Low Level Wind Shear Alert System
LMM	Locator Middle Marker
LNAV	Lateral Navigation
LNDG	Landing
LO	Locator at Outer Marker Site
LOC	Localizer
LOM	Locator Outer Marker
LONG	Longitude
LP	Localizer Performance
LPV	Localizer Performance with Vertical Guidance
LSALT	Lowest Safe Altitude
LT	Local Time
LTP	Landing Threshold Point
LTS	Lights
LTS	Lower Than Standard
LVP	Low Visibility Procedures
LWIS	Limited Weather Information System
M	Meters
MAA	Maximum Authorized Altitude
MACG	Missed Approach Climb Gradient
MAG	Magnetic
MAHF	Missed Approach Holding Fix
MALS	Medium Intensity Approach Light System
MALSF	Medium Intensity Approach Light System with Sequenced Flashing Lights

MALSR	Medium Intensity Approach Light System with Runway Alignment Indicator Lights	MTCA	Minimum Terrain Clearance Altitude
MAP	Missed Approach Point	MTMA	Military Terminal Control Area
MAX	Maximum	MTOM	Maximum Take-off Mass
MB	Millibars	MTOW	Maximum Take-off Weight
MCA	Minimum Crossing Altitude	MUN	Municipal
MCAF	Marine Corps Air Facility	MVA	Minimum Vectoring Altitude
MCAS	Marine Corps Air Station	N	Night, North or Northern
MCTA	Military Controlled Airspace	NA	Not Authorized
MDA	Minimum Descent Altitude	NAAS	Naval Auxiliary Air Station
MDA(H)	Minimum Descent Altitude (Height)	NADC	Naval Air Development Center
MDT	Mountain Daylight Time	NAEC	Naval Air Engineering Center
MEA	Minimum Enroute Altitude	NAF	Naval Air Facility
MEHT	Minimum Eye Height Over Threshold	NALF	Naval Auxiliary Landing Field
		NAP	Noise Abatement Procedure
MEML	Memorial	NAR	North American Routes
MET	Meteorological	NAS	Naval Air Station
MF	Mandatory Frequency	NAT	North Atlantic Traffic
MFA	Minimum Flight Altitude	NAT/OTS	North Atlantic Traffic/Organized Track System
MHA	Minimum Holding Altitude		
MHz	Megahertz	NATIONAL XXX	National Specific Criteria
MI	Medium Intensity (lights)		
MIALS	Medium Intensity Approach Light System	NATL	National
		NAVAID	Navigational Aid
MIL	Military	NCA	Northern Control Area
MIM	Minimum	NCN	NavData Change Notices
MIN	Minute	NCRP	Non-Compulsory Reporting Point
MIPS	Military Instrument Procedure Standardization	NDB	Non-Directional Beacon/Radio Beacon
MIRL	Medium Intensity Runway Edge Lights	NE	Northeast
		NM	Nautical Mile(s)
MKR	Marker Radio Beacon	No	Number
MLS	Microwave Landing System	NoPT	No Procedure Turn
MM	Middle Marker	NOTAM	Notices to Airmen
MNM	Minimum	NOTSP	Not Specified
MNPS	Minimum Navigation Performance Specifications	NPA	Non-Precision Approach
		NW	Northwest
MOA	Military Operation Area	NWC	Naval Weapons Center
MOC	Minimum Obstacle/Obstruction Clearance	OAC	Oceanic Area Control
		OAS	Obstacle Assessment Surface
MOCA	Minimum Obstruction Clearance Altitude	OCA	Oceanic Control Area
		OCA (H)	Obstacle Clearance Altitude (Height)
MORA	Minimum Off-Route Altitude (Grid or Route)		
		OCL	Obstacle Clearance Limit
MRA	Minimum Reception Altitude	OCNL	Occasional
MROT	Minimum Runway Occupancy Time	OCTA	Oceanic Control Area
		ODALS	Omni-Directional Approach Light System
MSA	Minimum Safe/Sector Altitude		
MSL	Mean Sea Level	ODP	Obstacle Departure Procedure
MST	Mountain Standard Time	OFZ	Obstacle Free Zone
MTA	Military Training Area	OM	Outer Marker
MTAF	Mandatory Traffic Advisory Frequency	OPS	Operations or Operates
		O/R	On Request

O/T	Other Times	RAIL	Runway Alignment Indicator Lights
OTR	Oceanic Transition Route	RAIM	Receiver Autonomous Integrity Monitoring
OTS	Other Than Standard		
OTS	Out-of-Service	RAPCON	Radar Approach Control
PA	Precision Approach	RASS	Remote Altimeter Source
PAL	Pilot Activated Lighting	RCAG	Remote Communications Air Ground
PANS-OPS	Procedures for Air Navigation Services - Aircraft Operations	RCC	Rescue Coordination Center
PAPI	Precision Approach Path Indicator	RCL	Runway Centerline
PAR	Precision Approach Radar	RCLM	Runway Center Line Markings
PARK	Parking	RCO	Remote Communications Outlet
PBN	Performance Based Navigation	REF	Reference
PCL	Pilot Controlled Lighting	REIL	Runway End Identifier Lights
PCN	Pavement Classification Number	REP	Reporting Point
PCZ	Positive Control Zone	RESA	Runway End Safety Area
PDC	Pre-Departure Clearance	REV	Reverse
PDG	Procedure Design Gradient	REP	Ramp Entrance Point
PDT	Pacific Daylight Time	RF	Radius to Fix
PERF	Performance	RL	Runway (edge) Lights
PERM	Permanent	RMZ	Radio Mandatory Zone
PinS	Point In Space	RNAV	Area Navigation
PISTON	Piston Aircraft	RNP	Required Navigation Performance
PJE	Parachute Jumping Exercise	RNP AR	Required Navigation Performance Authorization Required
PLASI	Pulsating Visual Approach Slope Indicator	RNPC	Required Navigation Performance Capability
PNR	Prior Notice Required	ROC	Rate of Climb
POFZ	Precision Obstacle Free Zone	RON	Remain Overnight
PPO	Prior Permission Only	RPT	Regular Public Transport
PPR	Prior Permission Required	RSA	Runway Safety Area
PRA	Precision Radar Approach	RTE	Route
PRM	Precision Radar Monitor	RTF	Radiotelephony
P-RNAV	Precision RNAV	RTS	Return to Service
PROC	Procedure	RVR	Runway Visual Range
PROP	Propeller Aircraft	RVSM	Reduced Vertical Separation Minimum
PSP	Pierced Steel Planking		
PST	Pacific Standard Time	RVV	Runway Visibility Values
PTO	Part Time Operation	RW	Runway
PVT	Private Operator	RWSL	Runway Status Lights
QDM	Magnetic bearing to facility	RWY	Runway
QDR	Magnetic bearing from facility	S	South or Southern
QFE	Height above airport elevation (or runway threshold elevation) based on local station pressure	SAAAR	Special Aircraft and Aircrew Authorization Required
		SALS	Short Approach Light System
QNE	Altimeter setting 29.92" Hg or 1013.2 Mb.	SALSF	Short Approach Light System with Sequenced Flashing Lights
QNH	Altitude above sea level based on local station pressure	SAP	Stabilized Approach
R	R-063 or 063R	SAR	Search and Rescue
	Magnetic Course (radial) measured as 063 from a VOR station. Flight can be inbound or outbound on this line.	SATCOM	Satellite voice air-ground calling
		SAWRS	Supplementary Aviation Weather Reporting Station
		SBAS	Satellite-Based Augmentation System
RA	Radio Altimeter		
RAI	Runway Alignment Indicator	SCA	Southern Control Area

184

SCOB	Scattered Clouds or Better	°T	True (degrees)
SDF	Simplified Directional Facility	T	Terrain clearance altitude (MOCA)
SDF	Step-Down Fix	T	Transmits only (radio frequencies)
SE	Southeast	T-VASI	Tee Visual Approach Slope Indicator
SEC	Seconds		
SELCAL	Selective Call System	TA	Transition Altitude
SFC	Surface of the earth (either land or water)	TAA	Terminal Arrival Area (FAA)
		TAA	Terminal Arrival Altitude (ICAO)
SFL	Sequenced Flashing Lights	TACAN	Tactical Air Navigation (bearing and distance station)
SFL-V	Sequenced Flashing Lights - Variable Light Intensity		
		TAR	Terminal Area Surveillance Radar
SID	Standard Instrument Departure	TAS	True Air Speed
SIWL	Single Isolated Wheel Load	TCA	Terminal Control Area
SKD	Scheduled	TCAS	Traffic Alert and Collision Avoidance System
SLP	Speed Limiting Point		
SM	Statute Miles	TCH	Threshold Crossing Height
SMA	Segment Minimum Altitude	TCTA	Transcontinental Control Area
SMGCS	Surface Movement Guidance and Control System	TDWR	Terminal Doppler Weather Radar
		TDZ	Touchdown Zone
SMSA	Segment Minimum Safe Altitude	TDZE	Touchdown Zone Elevation
SOC	Start of Climb	TEMP	Temporary
SODALS	Simplified Omnidirectional Approach Lighting System	TERPS	United States Standard for Terminal Instrument Procedure
SPAR	French Light Precision Approach Radar	THR	Threshold
		TIBA	Traffic Information Broadcast by Aircraft
SRA	Special Rules Area		
SRA	Surveillance Radar Approach	TIZ	Traffic Information Zone
SRE	Surveillance Radar Element	TL	Transition Level
SR-SS	Sunrise-Sunset	TMA	Terminal Control Area
SSALF	Simplified Short Approach Light System with Sequenced Flashing Lights	TML	Terminal
		TMN	Terminates
		TMZ	Transponder Mandatory Zone
SSALR	Simplified Short Approach Light System with Runway Alignment Indicator Lights	TNA	Transition Area
		TODA	Take-off Distance Available
		TORA	Take-off Run Available
SSALS	Simplified Short Approach Light System	TP	Turning Point
		TRA	Temporary Reserved Airspace
SSB	Single Sideband	TRACON	Terminal Radar Approach Control
SSR	Secondary Surveillance Radar (in U.S.A. ATCRBS)	TRANS	Transition(s)
		TRANS ALT	Transition Altitude
STAP	Parameter Automatic Transmission System	TRANS LEVEL	Transition Level
STAR	Standard Terminal Arrival Route (USA)		
		TRCV	Tri-Color Visual Approach Slope Indicator
	Standard Instrument Arrival (ICAO)		
STD	Indication of an altimeter set to 29.92" Hg or 1013.2 hPa (Mb) without temperature correction	TSA	Temporary Segregated Area
		TVOR	Terminal VOR
		TWEB	Transcribed Weather Broadcast
Std	Standard	TWIP	Terminal Weather Information for Pilots
ST-IN	Straight-in		
STOL	Short Take-off and Landing	TWR	Tower (Aerodrome Control)
SUPP	Supplemental/Supplementary	TWY	Taxiway
SW	Single Wheel Landing Gear	U	Unspecified
SW	Southwest	U	UNICOM
SYS	System	UAS	Unmanned Aerial System

UAV	Unmanned Aerial Vehicle	
UFN	Until Further Notice	
UHF	Ultra High Frequency (300-3000 MHz)	
UIR	Upper Flight Information Region	
UNCT'L	Uncontrolled	
UNICOM	Aeronautical Advisory Service	
UNICOM (A)	Automated UNICOM	
UNL	Unlimited	
UPR	User Preferred Route	
U/S	Unserviceable	
USAF	US Air Force	
USB	Upper Sideband	
USN	US Navy	
UTA	Upper Control Area	
UTC	Coordinated Universal Time	
VAL	Vertical Alert Limit	
VAR	Magnetic Variation	
VASI	Visual Approach Slope Indicator	
VDA	Vertical Descent Angle	
VDP	Visual Descent Point	
VE	Visual Exempted	
VFR	Visual Flight Rules	
VGSI	Visual Glide Slope Indicator	
VHA	Volcanic Hazard Area	
VHF	Very High Frequency (30-300 MHz)	
VIS	Visibility	
VMC	Visual Meteorological Conditions	
VNAP	Vertical Noise Abatement Procedures	
VNAV	Vertical Navigation	
VOLMET	Meteorological Information for Aircraft in Flight	
VOR	VHF Omnidirectional Range	
VORTAC	VOR and TACAN co-located	
VOT	Radiated Test Signal VOR	
VPA	Vertical Path Angle	
VPT	Visual Maneuvering with Prescribed Tracks	
VSS	Visual Segment Surface	
VV	Vertical Visibility	
V/V	Vertical Velocity or speed	
W	West or Western	
WAAS	Wide Area Augmentation System	
WATIR	Weather and Terminal Information Reciter	
WH	Western Hemisphere	
W/O	Without	
WP	Area Navigation (RNAV) Waypoint	
WSP	Weather Systems Processor	
WX	Weather	
X	Communication Frequency On Request	
Z	Zulu Time/Coordinated Universal Time (UTC)	

Symbols

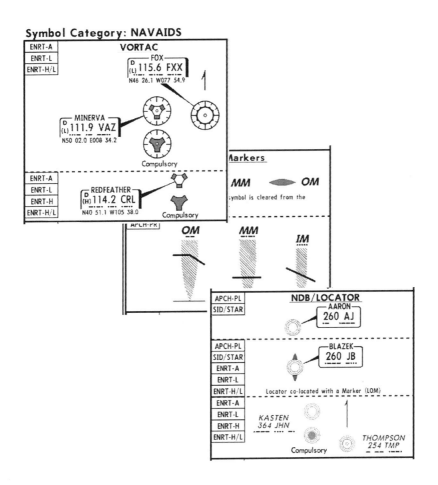

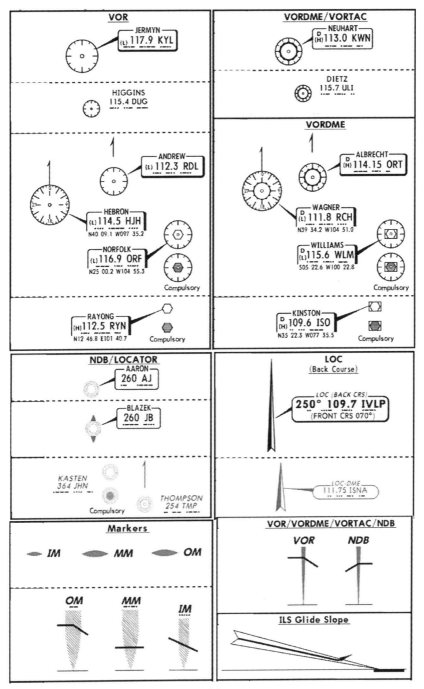

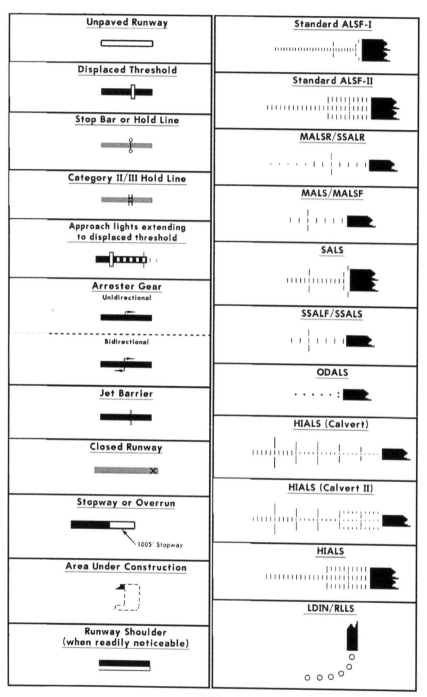

Holding Patterns	DME and DME Radial Formation
	D →
Intercept Route	**Non Precision Final Approach Fix**
BATT INTERCEPTS →	✳
	Non Precision Missed Approach Fix
	M

Non-Compulsory	Standard ALSF-I
△ △	ALSF-I
△ △	
Compulsory	**Standard ALSF-II**
▲ ▲ ▲	ALSF-II
▲ ▲ ▲	
RNAV Non-Compulsory	**MALSR**
✦	MALSR
RNAV Compulsory	**SSALR**
✦ ✦	SSALR
Mileage Break/CNF Non-Compulsory Fix	**MALS**
×	MALS
	MALSF
	MALSF
Fly Over Fix Indicated by circle around fix	**SALS**
⊛ ⊙ ⊕	SALS
Meteorological Report Point	**SSALF**
Ⓜ	SSALF

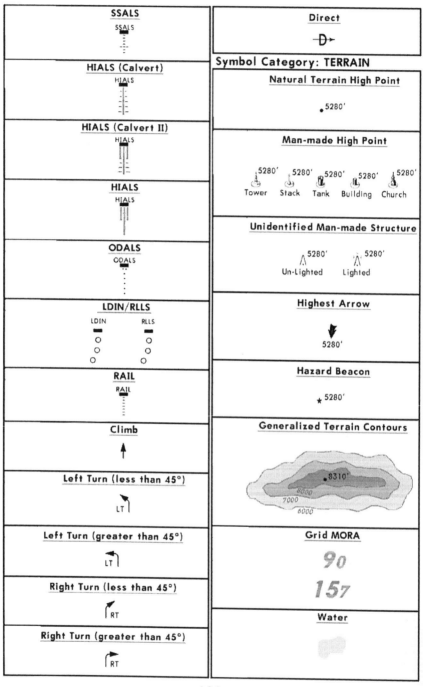

Track/Airway	Altitude Change "T"
→ → → - - - - - - - - - - Overlying High Altitude Airway	MEA, MAA, MOCA, or MORA change. Does not apply to GPS MEA's or at Navaids ⊣
Diversionary Route — — — — —	**Total Mileage** Total Mileage between Navaids ⟨23⟩
Non-precision when charted with precision approach — — — —	**Change Over Point** Mileages indicate point to change Navaids 22 ⌐ 65
Arrival/Departure Route — — →	**Even and Odd Indicators** Even and Odd altitudes are used in direction indicated ⟨E E⟩ ⟨O O⟩ ⟨E&O E&O⟩ E&O
Transition Track - - - - - - →	**Prior Permission Required** Prior Permission Required from ATC for flight in direction of arrow. ◄PPR
High Level Approach Track • • • • • • • • • • •	**Flight Planned Route** FPR►
Visual Track →-→-→-→	**Airway By-Pass** ⌒
VNAV/VDA Vertical descent angle and/or path ∙∙∙∙∙∙∙∙∙∙∙∙∙ Vertical descent angle and/or path to DA for approved operators — — — —	**Airway Designator** Negative ■V 102■ Positive □U 571□
Radar Vectors ►►►►►►►►►►►►	**Route Suffix** Suffixes are added to indicate more restrictive segment along airway. Each suffix has a unique meaning. □J 225□■R■
Missed Approach Course — — — — — →	
Navigational Signal Gap ■ ■	**One Way Airway** ◄■V 76■

Manufactured by Amazon.ca
Bolton, ON